BIBLICAL GREEK

A SIMPLIFIED APPROACH TO THE LANGUAGE OF THE NEW TESTAMENT

DR CHARLES VOGAN

Cover – Codex Vaticanus

ISBN 978-1-935969-15-0

Ravenbrook Publishers

A subsidiary of
Shenandoah Bible Ministries

www.Ravenbrook.org

CONTENTS

PREFACE

This grammar on Biblical Greek is designed to give the absolute beginner a fair mastery of the basics of Greek. But if you would compare it to many other grammars available, you'll notice that many of the details are missing. This is for two reasons:

First, I felt that keeping things simple, and limiting the study to the broad principles of Greek grammar, would be the best way for many students to get introduced to the language. Learning often happens best when we back up and look at the most important points first – and *master them* – before we go on to examine details. It helps to get the general lay of the land first, the peaks and the valleys, before starting to map out individual fields.

Second, most students of Greek (even pastors!) aren't going to use the language to any great extent. Their purpose will be primarily to help them understand particular passages in the Greek New Testament. Since only a Greek scholar can pick up the New Testament and read anywhere without resorting to language helps, why spend so much time on details that one will forget anyway? The student of the Greek New Testament will want to have a lexicon handy, and a full grammatical reference work, if he hopes to wade through the endless exceptions, rare words, and difficult syntax. We may as well lay a basic foundation now for general grammatical rules, and leave the complexity of the language for the student when he works through a particular passage.

Besides, learning New Testament Greek can be fun. By keeping to the broad, simple principles, we can keep that spirit of enjoyment – much of the New Testament *really is* this simple to work with.

BIBLICAL GREEK

The Old Testament was written in Hebrew, but the New Testament was written in Greek. The disciples of Jesus spoke Aramaic, as did Jesus; but when it came time to record the life and sayings of their Lord, they used the one language that all the then-known world knew – Greek. Not the flowering, philosophical, or artistic Greek of the scholars, but what was known as '*koine*' Greek – the 'vulgar' tongue of the common people. Like the incarnation, the message of Jesus was brought to the level of the lowliest upon earth.

Of course, no one speaks this ancient language now. Modern Greek is the result of 2000 years of inevitable change, and the two resemble each other very little. So the New Testament is one of the few surviving witnesses of that noble language.

Noble it is, too. Though it was the everyday speech of the marketplace and home, it could carry the eternal and glorious message of the ages with beauty and simplicity. In the hands of John the beloved disciple, the Gospel is told in a simple and humble idiom. In the hands of the scholar Paul, the theology of the Church is laid out with words of precision and often-times difficult sentence structure. Each author spoke differently, with different levels of ability and different backgrounds. But the Scriptures took form as an impressive array of truth in history's most remarkable piece of literature, all in the common man's language.

We must remember that *koine* Greek is a different language than ours. As in the study of any language, we're going to have some problems understanding Greek in at least two areas:

Word Meaning. In the following lessons each word will usually have only one or two meanings assigned to it. But once you begin using your own dictionary, you'll find a bewildering list of possible meanings for most words. Remember that *koine* Greek was a living language, like English is now; please allow it room for growth and application. The English word 'run' may mean 1) to move one's legs quickly forward, over and over, 2) to operate a vehicle, 3) to drip down, 4) to separate, as in nylons running; the list could go on. Greek words are often the same way; finding a word's proper meaning is usually done by looking at the context of the word and using your best judgment. Then maybe you'll appreciate the many efforts at translating the Bible!

Idiom. Idiom is a special way of saying something that doesn't quite mean what it literally says. Every language is full of peculiar idioms. In English we say, "Let's run down to the store," though we don't intend to run nor does the store have to be 'down' from us geographically. In John 2:4 the Greek literally says, "What to you and to me, woman?" We English readers react with "What an awkward way of saying it!" But we're the outsiders; the Greeks talked the way they wanted to talk, and if we want to understand them then we have to learn not only their words but the *way* they used those words.

The grammar of Greek is pretty straightforward; it's just a matter of using patterns and forms. If you can get yourself ready for the unexpected and often mysterious word meanings and idioms, then you won't have any problem at all in learning Greek.

You need an incentive to learn Greek; and if you don't have one yet, let me give you one — you can read the Scriptures in their original language. There are real benefits in being able to do this.

- When you know how to read Greek for yourself you're no longer chained to the work of other men. To be sure, the Greek scholars of history have done staggering amounts of work for the Church just so we could have the Bible in our mother tongue. And some of the translations that we have are masterful productions. But if you can read the Greek New Testament for yourself you'll find worlds of meaning and insight that are impossible to pack into a single translation. Often a word looks uninteresting in English; but the Greek word behind it unfolds a veritable drama before our eyes. For example, in 2 Peter 2:1 we find the word 'Lord'. Did you know that here, instead of using the Greek word that's always used for 'Lord' elsewhere in the New Testament, Peter uses the rarely-used word δεσπότης, 'despotes', from which we get our word 'despot'? That throws a very interesting light on the whole passage, which the English never even gives us a clue of.

- There's the psychological benefit of being able to read the very words that the apostles wrote. That really closes the gap between their world and ours. This strange tongue used to be a distant world, only made real to us by someone else's educated opinions. We were only allowed to look through the translator's windows, so to speak. With the Greek we can sit down with the men of the Bible and listen in on what they're saying.

- There's a mental discipline required in learning Greek. These lessons were designed to be as simple as possible, arranging the material in an easy-to-learn format without a lot of the unnecessary trappings of a more formal grammar. But as easy as that may sound, it still requires work. You must put your mind to the task with a determination to learn the lessons well. At first it may seem too exacting and difficult; but persistence always brings achievements. We finish a job only by working at it. Then when you start to master the language, you'll begin to appreciate the people of times past who learned to read by using only their Bibles.

- Probably the most important result in learning Greek is that you'll be working so closely and painstakingly with the Scriptures that you'll get a much deeper understanding of its message. Just reading the English version often isn't very beneficial; we tend to run over many deep connections in the text unawares and miss out on thought-provoking meditations. In learning Greek, however, you'll be forced to study the relationships of every word and phrase to the on-going thought of the passage. You can't miss much of its spiritual teachings when you're working that carefully.

Hopefully these will be good enough reasons to motivate you to study *koine* Greek. Perhaps you have your own. In any case, once you've started and keep at it, you can't fail to be rewarded. Greek may not be the language of Heaven, but it's the vessel of the inspired story of the Lord's life and teachings in this world. That's a beautiful and faith-building story in any language!

A SHORT HISTORY OF THE TEXT OF THE NEW TESTAMENT

Materials

The writers of the New Testament books didn't have it nearly as easy as modern writers do. Writing was a chore, at least as far as the materials were concerned. They used feathered quills, split reeds sharpened to a point, or wooden styles for a pen. Their ink was a carbon or ground-mineral mixture that yielded black or brown tint. For paper they had several choices: most used the **papyrus** stem by splitting it and laying the pieces side by side, and gluing some pieces on the back to hold the whole thing together. Some used **parchment**, which was dried and scraped animal skin. At first the papyrus or parchment pages were stuck together end to end and rolled up into a scroll. Although it was handy to carry, it was difficult to use, because one had to unroll it all the way back to the place that was wanted. Later, in the second century A.D., the **codex** was invented; it was the forerunner of the modern book, in that its separate leaves were sewn together along one edge.

Autographs

The New Testament writers each wrote their books with particular churches in mind; they weren't really designed to be kept around for centuries. So, although we would dearly love to see those original copies or **autographs** of the New Testament books, we probably never will. The papyrus or parchment has probably long since crumbled into dust through neglect.

But the Church of Christ lives by those inspired letters. The history of the text of the New Testament has been that of a search for the earliest manuscripts, the ones closest in time to the original letters. Our doctrine of the inspiration of the Scriptures is that the autographs of the books were inerrant (free from any errors) and inspired by God, every word of them. So it's important that our Greek texts of today follow as closely as possible (as closely as we can determine) the texts of the autographs of the books.

Copying manuscripts

Immediately after the original books were written, some of the Christians from other churches wanted copies too; and as the word got around in a neighborhood of churches that a letter from an apostle was in town, many others wanted a copy of their own to read and study. So the need arose to copy the new Testament books.

Some churches hired scribes to do this tedious work; it was all done by hand, since the printing press was yet to be invented some 1400 years down the road. Sometimes the scribes were Christians and sometimes they weren't; some copies, therefore, got loving care, while others didn't fare so well.

Soon the autographs were no longer available, being either lost or destroyed. Providentially, copies existed by now in many places throughout the civilized world; and wherever the Gospel was carried, the New Testament was there and in great demand. Copies sprang up everywhere, and soon copies of copies were being made.

The Canon

There were many other books being circulated at that time that competed for a place in the Scriptures of the Church. So many of these were obviously false that after a couple of hundred years Christians became alarmed. Which are the true writings of the apostles? they asked. After a hundred years of debate, indecision and concern, there arose by common consensus the list of 27 books that we now recognize; these are the true, sacred writings, the early Christians decided. By 367 A.D. the 27-book list was known by all, and in 393 A.D. a church council affirmed that the Church seemed to have accepted these as the true Scriptures.

Variant readings

There was only one problem to this practice of copying manuscripts: the new copy was almost sure to contain copying errors. For many reasons the copy would often end up reading slightly differently than the original. Here are some of the reasons:

- weariness (scribes usually stood to write)
- skipping words
- accidentally adding extra words
- accidentally misspelling (this was especially the case of someone was reading the manuscript aloud and several scribes copied what they heard)
- recopying whole lines accidentally
- mistaking marginal comments in the original to be words of the text itself

Once a new copy had an error, any copies made from it in the future would have the same error. In this way, after a while, errors were compounded at alarming rates throughout the centuries until, now, we don't have an exact idea of how the autographs read word for word. But it isn't as bad as it sounds; the errors were almost always minor; and though many *variant readings* (or different word-for-word readings among the manuscripts existing today) exist for many texts in the New Testament, none of them call for any change of the doctrine of the Church.

The important point of variant readings is this: we have to use the testimony of the earliest manuscripts, or the ones closest to the autographs, since theoretically they would have less errors than later manuscripts. However, one must sometimes resort to the newer ones when the earlier manuscripts disagree among themselves.

Here's a hypothetical situation in which an original copy in a certain country was used to make other copies. Note how a group of manuscripts will have the same errors, and another group will have its own errors, and so on (M1 means the first error made, M2 the second error, etc.).

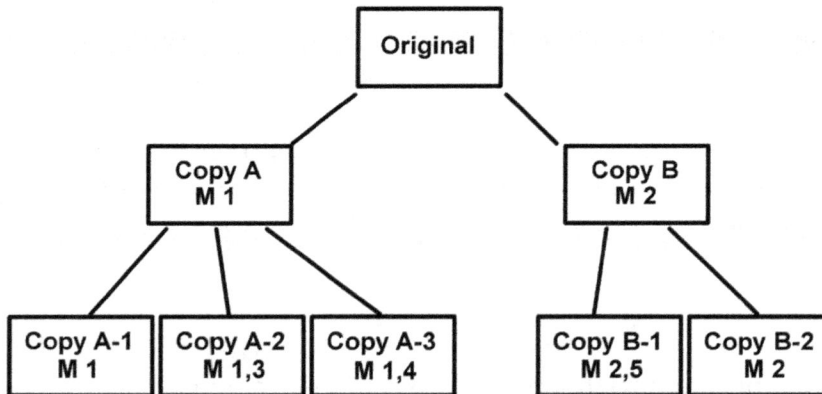

```
                        Original
              /                        \
        Copy A                          Copy B
         M 1                             M 2
      /    |    \                       /    \
 Copy A-1 Copy A-2 Copy A-3      Copy B-1 Copy B-2
  M 1     M 1,3    M 1,4          M 2,5    M 2
```

Let's say that someone made two copies of the **Original** and sent them to two different cities: **Copy A** and **Copy B**. The problem is that **Copy A** had a mistake in it — **M1** — and **Copy B** had a different mistake in it — **M2**. Then each church in each city decided to make additional copies. From **Copy A** came **Copy A-1**, **Copy A-2**, and **Copy A-3** — all of which have the same mistake **M1** in them. And in the process of copying, **Copy A-2** picked up an additional mistake **M3** and **Copy A-3** has a mistake **M4**. Meanwhile, in the second church, they made **Copy B-1** and **Copy B-2** from their copy. And **Copy B-1** got a new error **M5**.

Families form

Although the number of books was finally decided on, the actual texts of the books were far from being identical. Since the Scriptures were carried to many different places in the Roman Empire and beyond, the copies made of the original in any one place tended to resemble each other in how they read and, subsequently, looked less like copies of other groups somewhere else. Eventually *families of manuscripts* came into existence, resembling each other closely but differing from other families in predictable ways. Families of manuscripts, then, collected in certain geographical locations.

Each family of manuscripts was used for the production of translations into other languages; the Coptic Bible, the Arabic Bible, and the Syriac Bible each came from a different family of manuscripts. That's why the problem of variant readings becomes so complex: these translations aren't only different in language, but their original Greek parent manuscripts were different as well. To compare these foreign versions with our existing Greek manuscripts, one must take that fact into consideration too.

The centers of the main families of Greek manuscripts were:

Alexandrian Family, around Alexandria, Egypt
Caesarean Family, around Caesarea in Palestine
Byzantine Family, around Constantinople
Western Family, around Rome

Unfortunately, the Caesarean family has proved to be not so reliable; the Byzantine is a little better (but it's a later family than the others and thus has more errors): the Alexandrian and Western families are the most reliable. One must remember, too, that each family took shape at a different time from the others; time of origin obviously affects its reliability. It's a very complicated business.

There are at present thousands of Greek manuscripts in existence, though most of them are only parts of the New Testament. No other ancient book of history has so many copies still around. Most of them are manuscripts written later than the eighth century; only a few hundred manuscripts that exist are from the second to the seventh century.

Textus Receptus

In 1515 Erasmus, a distinguished Catholic scholar, published the first machine-printed Greek Bible. He mainly used two Byzantine manuscripts that were copied in the twelfth century. They were missing a few texts here and there; so he made up some of them by filling in with translations from his Latin Bible! An example of his inaccuracy is in Acts 9:6. Paul's question is found in the Latin Bible but is found in no existing Greek manuscript – but now it's in the KJV. Another error is 1 John 5:7, which is only found in three late manuscripts and the Latin Bible. It's actually an addition to the text made by a Franciscan friar in 1520 and reluctantly added by Erasmus to later editions of his Bible.

In 1527 Erasmus produced his final edition of the Greek Bible; in it he used several other Byzantine texts to make some changes. In 1550 Robert Stephanus issued his own Greek Bible based largely on Erasmus' version but with some changes. In the Latin advertisement of one of Stephanus' editions was the blurb that this was "the text which is now received ('textus receptus') by all, in which we give nothing changed or corrupted (from former Stephanus editions)." So the advertising by-line became the revered name for history's most famous edition of the Greek Bible.

The King James Bible

In 1604 King James of England was reviewing what could be done to improve the general condition of the Church of England when someone suggested that a new translation be made of the Bible. James was taken with the idea, and he made it an official enterprise. Fifty four scholars were collected to work on the translation. In 1611 they finally finished their work and presented it to the king as the patron of the project. It was decreed that the new translation would take the place of the many others floating around at that time as the official (or "authorized" – that is, by the King himself) Bible to be read in the churches. Thus the King James Version entered history.

The KJV was a beautiful piece of literature. It captured the poetry and grace of the original Scriptures much better than its contemporaries; and its adaptability to memorization work made it certain to be a favorite. The translation itself is a good blend of literal and idiomatic methods.

Like any new translation, however, it had its shortcomings. For one thing, it's based on the Textus Receptus, so it picked up all the problems that are inherent in that text, like the Latin fill-ins and the spurious texts of 1 Jn. 5 and Acts 9:6. Some other interesting foibles show up. One of the early editions of the KJV printed the name 'Jesus' in Acts 7:45 and Hebrews 4:8 (it should have been 'Joshua' - the Hebrew name 'Yehoshua' can be translated either way). Also, if you look carefully, there are paragraph notations (¶) throughout the KJV until you get to Acts 20:36 where they suddenly disappear, never to be used again. Perhaps the thought of Paul's skull-cracking logic in the upcoming books discouraged the editors!

Finally, in Matthew 23:24 a typographical error in one of the early editions has survived to this day: it should read "strain *out* a gnat" instead of "strain *at* a gnat".

Modern manuscript research

Since the days of the KJV, work has been going on in the field of Greek manuscripts. During the last century some amazing finds greatly changed the whole question of an authoritative Greek text. Unknown to Erasmus or the KJV translators, these early manuscripts let us reach back more than a thousand years further in antiquity to within a century or two of the autographs.

In 1881 two English scholars, Westcott and Hort, published a new Greek text to replace the Textus Receptus, based on the newest manuscript evidence; it was mainly from Alexandrian sources. In 1898 Eberhard Nestle published an *eclectic* Greek text; that means that he didn't follow any one family of manuscripts but, according to some sound and sensible rules, chose what were the most likely readings from a variety of manuscripts. Revisions of Nestle's text continued into our century. Then in 1966 Aland, Black, Metzger and Wikgren put together a new eclectic text that reflected the twentieth century's most recent manuscript finds. It's now used in most of the translating work in the Bible Societies.

Modern versions

When the break was finally made from the Textus Receptus, some daring individuals came out with new English translations to be used instead of the KJV. The Revised Version (1881) was the contribution of the English, and the American Standard Version (1901) took shape here in America. Then in 1946 the Revised Standard Version was published; it was a scholarly work representing the best of textual research. The New American Standard (1960) was a revision of the ASV; it's extremely literal and idiomatically rigid. In 1961 the New English Bible was issued in England; not very literal and too idiomatic and free. Recently the United Bible Society published the New International Version (1973), a real attempt at putting the Greek into common everyday language; it blends literal and idiomatic translation, and captures the poetry and glory of the original. It was intended to be the "KJV" of our day.

A word should be said here about modern translations. A language consists of words and idiomatic phrases; literal meanings and implied meanings. A faithful translation will take both seriously and try to reflect exactly what the original is saying. That's not easy. There have been many attempts at this, some successful and many not so successful. If the more popular translations are put on a scale showing how literal or idiomatic they are, it might look like this:

```
   NASB ESV KJV NIV              NEB      TEV     LB
  |                                                      |
Fully                                                 Fully
Literal                                            Idiomatic
```

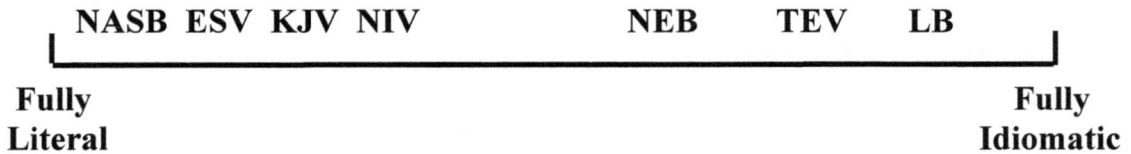

NASB — *New American Standard Bible*
ESV — *English Standard Version*
KJV — *King James Version*
NIV — *New International Version*
NEB — *New English Bible*
TEV — *Today's English Version*
LB — *Living Bible* (Strictly speaking, this isn't a translation but a paraphrase. Ken Taylor put the King James Version into his own words. This accounts for it being so idiomatic.)

The question has been raised, should we have new translations? Isn't the KJV good enough for us, seeing how God has used it so powerfully in the past?

First of all, the advocates of the KJV either don't know Greek or they're ignoring the fundamental question. The manuscript problem alone warrants us to find a better Greek text than the Textus Receptus; and when we've found those texts then we need new translations. Furthermore, the KJV's answer for many texts, although good, is only one possibility out of many – some of them much better than its choice. The flexibility of the Greek allows for that.

Second, although the KJV was an exceptionally good translation in its day, and certainly has been used by God through the centuries, it's quickly losing its usability in our own time. Linguists tell us that a people's language changes about 5% every century; that means that in the last 400 years almost 20% of the KJV's English has become obsolete to us. We just don't talk that way now. We could continue to use the KJV, but time is quickly eroding away our understanding of its style of English.

Third, since it's becoming increasingly difficult to understand, the younger generation is equating the KJV with tradition, superstition, and ultra- conservatism. In an age of such a vast group of unchurched, anti-religious young people, we need to reach them with an intelligible speech.

Fourth, in the light of the need on one hand, and the vast manuscript wealth and research results on the other, it would be a crime not to render the Message of the Ages into the language of the common people. The New Testament was first written in *koine* Greek, the language of the market-place and home. Are we not also responsible to bring that message to our market-places and homes, in our own language of our own time, so that men and women will understand and see the Lord that it speaks of? Shouldn't we use what God has so graciously provided for us – the light of manuscript finds – and speak intelligibly to our families and friends? Why hold ourselves to Shakespearean dialect for tradition's sake?

The work of the Lord goes on. His Providence has always supplied his people with his Word to protect them and teach them. New translations will be made in the future, and further study will yield more valuable finds. Let's hope that we can catch that vision and share the '*koine*' message to our own age.

MAKING A NOTEBOOK

I would strongly urge you to keep a notebook as you work with your Greek Bible. There are several reasons for this:

It makes a more studious, or serious, atmosphere as you're studying, and you'll end up doing a lot better job translating. If your notebook is kept up-to-date and pretty complete, it represents a lot of work on your part and should motivate you to keep working at it.

It will prove to be an invaluable aid to you in the future – there's nothing that will be so satisfying to you as when, ten years down the road, you're wondering what you came up with on a certain Greek text and you dig up your exhaustive analysis of the Greek.

The sheer regimen of keeping the notebook will result in quite a valuable study for you. You'll be amazed at how the meaning of your text will gradually unfold into a living message – and it never would have happened if you hadn't dug so deeply into the original.

There are different ways you could arrange your notebook. I'll show you an example to give you an idea of what I'm talking about:

John 1

Location	word	analysis	meaning
1:1	ἐν	preposition, no endings	"in"
1:1	ἀρχῇ	noun, 1st decl., f.s.d.	"beginning, origin"
1:1	ἦν	verb, imperfect, 3rd p.s.	"was"

(**Notes:** The first word is a preposition which doesn't use special case endings; meaning in this case is pretty straightforward.

The second word, a noun, is a word of the first declension, feminine, singular, and in the dative case. Its meaning is made more interesting by the allusion to the "origin" of the world.

The third word is a verb, tense = imperfect, third person, singular.)

This is how it can be done. Then every once in a while you should stop and translate what you've worked through so far, as best as you can (but don't try to be a scholar about it – you'll lose the fun of it!). Don't look to an English translation! Do what you can first, on your own; then get something to help you if you need it. And be sure to put your translation in your notebook too. And please, don't try to translate the Greek as closely to the KJV or NIV or another translation as you can remember it. Remember, you're studying Greek to enable you to make up your own mind on what it says; if all that you're going to do is copy the KJV, then there's no use to study Greek!

THE GREEK ALPHABET

	Capital letter	Small letter	Name of letter	Pronunciation of letter
Vowel	A	α	alpha	a as in *father*
	B	β	beta	b as in *boy*
	Γ	γ	gamma	g as in *gone*
	Δ	δ	delta	d as in *did*
Vowel	E	ϵ	epsilon	e as in *pepsi*
	Z	ζ	zeta	z as in *zoo*
Vowel	H	η	eta	e as in *they*
	Θ	θ	theta	th as in *thought*
Vowel	I	ι	iota	i as in *sit*
	K	κ	kappa	k as in *kin*
	Λ	λ	lamda	l as in *lamb*
	M	μ	mu	m as in *man*
	N	ν	nu	n as in *new*
	Ξ	ξ	xi	x as in *vex*
Vowel	O	o	omicron	o as in *on*
	Π	π	pi	p as in *pin*

	P	ρ	rho	r as in *run*
	Σ	σ	sigma	s as in *sell*
	T	τ	tau	t as in *tag*
Vowel	Υ	υ	upsilon	u as in *euu* *
	Φ	φ	phi	ph as in *phoney*
	X	χ	chi	ch as in *Achtung* *
	Ψ	ʊ	psi	ps as in *lips*
Vowel	Ω	ω	omega	o as in *home*

The **Υ, υ** is like the sound you would make when you're disgusted with something.

The **X, χ** is like the sound you would make in the back of your throat when you're going to spit.

Notes:

Each letter is pronounced only one way – as shown. Greek isn't like English where you can have many different pronunciations for a single letter.

σ is written when a sigma begins or is inside a word. **ς** is only written when it's the very last letter of the word. For example –

$$σίγμα \qquad πίστις \qquad Θεός$$

Diphthongs

When certain pairs of vowels occur in a word, they're pronounced as one sound. Any other pairs of vowels are not diphthongs; they're supposed to be pronounced as two separate vowels. Here's a listing of all the Greek diphthongs and how to pronounce them:

αι	ai as in aisle
ει	ei as in weight
οι	oi as in boil
υι	uee as in queen
αυ	ow as in owl
ευ	tough one: ew as in Edward, only say it without the d!
ου	ou as in soup
ηυ	ayw as in wayward
ωυ	another tough one: try saying a long o and quickly put a long u on the end

Exercise

Write the capital and small letters of the Greek alphabet. Then write the name of each letter beside it, only write the name using Greek letters. For example, start with A –

A   α   αλφα

FIRST CLASS WORDS – NOUNS

Types of words

There are three types of words in the Greek language: [1]

- *First class words:*   these name, identify, or describe something
- *Second class words:*   these are the action words, the doers in the sentence
- *Third class words:*   these are auxiliary words, or helpers

The parts of speech break down into the three classes like this:

First class	Second class	Third class
nouns	verbs	conjunctions
pronouns		adverbs
adjectives		prepositions
articles		

It helps to group the types of words together like this; we can learn the special characteristics of each group easily and spot them immediately in a sentence.

Word endings

In English, almost always, you can tell what kind of word you're looking at by its position in the sentence. For example, if the word comes at the beginning of the sentence, it's the subject. If the word follows the subject then it's the verb. A direct object is at the end of a sentence. A preposition sits before its object, adverbs cling to their verbs, and adjectives stay close to nouns.

---

[1] I'm not referring to the *function* of a word – there are many kinds of functions that words serve in Greek. Rather I'm talking about *what we do* to the word – the prefixes and suffixes that we stick on the beginning and end. Grammarians don't usually divide the words up like this into three categories; but I felt it would be helpful for memorizing, because for example the first class words have much in common with each other and almost nothing in common with verbs. In this light there really are only three kinds of words in Greek!

But many languages don't have this peculiar characteristic, at least not to the extent that English has. You can't rearrange a sentence like "the dog bit the boy" without coming up with something silly: "The boy bit the dog." But you *can* rearrange the parts of a Greek sentence without changing its meaning. The reason for this is because almost every word in Greek has a special ending that makes it impossible to lose in the sentence. You know which word is the subject – no matter where it is – because it has a subject ending.

Right now we're going to look at a first class word – the **Noun**. Every noun can have many different endings attached to it, depending on the job that it's doing in the sentence. So let's look at noun endings and what they're like.

A noun ending will tell us three things about that noun. These three things are:

Gender. Gender is a carry-over from old days when people used to associate everything with the sexes. That is, one object seemed to them to have manly, or *masculine*, characteristics. Something else reminded them of womanly, or *feminine*, characteristics. And some things seemed to be neither – so they were *neuter*. Now we have three genders, and every noun has one. But a noun can have **only one** gender; it's either a masculine, feminine, or neuter noun.

Number. This means whether a noun is singular or plural. For example, you can have "the boy" (sing.) or "the boys" (pl.).

Case. This is what the noun's job is in the sentence. A noun can have any of the following jobs in a sentence:

> the **subject** – *Nominative* case
>
> showing **possession** – *Genitive* case
>
> the **indirect object** – *Dative* case
>
> the **direct object** – *Accusative* case

(There are other jobs and cases, but this will do for now.)

Declining nouns

Now, we have to put all this together. There are three facts that an ending tells us (gender, number, case), but there are a lot of possible endings that tell us these facts. So to lay out all the possible endings that a noun may have and still show the three facts of an ending, we have to have an orderly arrangement of the endings. This is called a *declension*.

	<u>Singular</u>	<u>Plural</u>
Nominative	-ος	-οι
Genitive	-ου	-ων
Dative	-ῳ	-οις
Accusative	-ον	-ους

(**Note:** That little iota under the dative singular ending is called an *iota subscript* – fancy name! At one time there used to be an iota in the word itself followed by an omega; but after a while it wasn't pronounced anymore. So rather than leave the iota where it was – the Greeks never kept any unnecessary letters in their words – or even drop it altogether, they put a tiny iota under the omega to remind them that it used to be there.)

Let's look at this declension. In grid fashion it gives us each ending for a noun, and the three facts that each ending represents. But where is the gender, you ask? The case and number are obvious, but you can't figure out the gender. Well, these are the **masculine** endings – feminine and neuter nouns have a different set of endings which we'll look at later. So, if you should find a noun with one of these endings on it, you can assume that it's a masculine noun. By the way, these are called the *second declension* endings.

Let's decline a noun, or put it into the grid of the masculine endings. First let's take the word Θεός, or "God", and get it down to the stem:

Θεός ; stem = θε-

Now let's stick each ending onto the stem:

	Singular	Plural
Nom:	Θεός	Θεοί
Gen:	Θεοῦ	Θεῶν
Dat.:	Θεῷ	Θεοῖς
Acc.:	Θεόν	Θεούς

(**Note:** To get the stem of a noun, look up the dictionary form – in this case you'd find "**Θεός, -ου m. – God**" in the dictionary – and just cut off the -ου of the genitive ending. There's your stem. The reason why you can't use the Nominative form of the noun to get the stem is that often the Nominative form of the word is spelled radically different from the rest of the forms.)

Let's practice. Which forms from the above declension would you use for the subject in a sentence?

Θεός (sing.) or θεοί (pl.)

Which form would be a direct object, singular?

Θεόν

How about "God's", a possessive form?

Θεοῦ

Learn these endings by heart, declining the noun Θεός over and over. You can then decline any second declension noun and recognize it in a sentence, and know the three facts about that noun.

Vocabulary

Nouns

ἄνθρωπος, -ου, m.	man
Θεός, -οῦ, m.	God
κόσμος, -ου, m.	world
Ἰάκωβος, -ου, m.	James
Ἰησοῦς, -ου, m.	Jesus
λόγος, -ου, m.	word
νόμος, -ου, m.	law
Πέτρος, -ου, m.	Peter
Χριστός, -οῦ, m.	Christ

(**Note:** The first entry is the noun in the nominative ending; the second is the genitive ending by itself – which tells you the declension (second) that this noun uses; the third is the gender; the last is the meaning. This is called the "dictionary form" of the noun.)

Verbs

ἀγαπά	he, she, or it loves
ἀγαπούσιν	they love
ἐστίν	he, she, or it is
εἰσίν	they are

Adjectives

καλός	good
πονηρός	bad
νεκρός	dead
ἅγιος	holy

Other words

καί	and

(**Note**: You'll notice that there's an aspiration mark (either ' or ') over the first letter of every word that begins with a vowel. This mark tells you whether to pronounce the vowel the way it is (') or to put an "h" sound (') in front of the vowel as you pronounce it. For example, pronounce ἄνθρωπος as "anthropos"; ἅγιος as "hagios.")

(**Note**: You'll also notice that there is one of three kinds of marks (at least) over just about every Greek word. (Either ´ or ` or ˆ). These are accents – they show you which syllable to stress when pronouncing the word. There are complicated rules for deciding where the accents go; we won't go into all that here. Just notice where they are and stress the appropriate syllable.)

You will find exercises for this lesson on page: 103

FIRST CLASS WORDS – NOUNS (PART 2)

Neuter Nouns

In the last lesson we looked at the declension, a way of arranging noun endings in a chart. These noun endings tell us the gender, number, and case of the noun, whatever they might be in the sentence.

But the endings we looked at are the second declension endings for **masculine** nouns. There are other sets of endings as well. For example, many **neuter** nouns share most of the same endings of the masculine second declension. The differences weren't enough to create a new declension, so these neuter nouns are called second declension nouns too. Here are the neuter endings:

	Singular	**Plural**
Nominative	-oν	-α
Genitive	-oυ	-ων
Dative	-ῳ	-οις
Accusative	-oν	-α

Notice that the only differences between these endings and the masculine endings are the Nominative and Accusative, singular and plural. All second declension neuters use these endings. But notice something else about neuter endings: the Accusative ending is identical to the Nominative ending. The plural endings are always **-α**, but the singular endings won't always be **-oν**; they will match each other, though, whatever they may be.

Here's the word for "child" declined:

τεκνόν; stem = τεκν-

	Singular	Plural
Nom:	τεκνόν	τεκνά
Gen:	τεκνοῦ	τεκνῶν
Dat.:	τεκνῷ	τεκνοῖς
Acc.:	τεκνόν	τεκνά

First Declension nouns

The first declension is made up mainly of feminine nouns (with a few exceptions). Of course the first declension endings are different than the second declension endings; so you should be able to spot them right away. And we'll arrange these endings into a ***paradigm*** (PAIR-ah-dime – it means an orderly chart of the declension) in a minute. But first we need to look at an oddity about these first declension nouns.

The second declension nouns were easy to decline. One just needed to knock off the Genitive ending of the dictionary form, and using this stem add the declension endings. But that's because almost all of those nouns ended the same way in the Nominative form.

First declension nouns, if grouped together according to their characteristics, end in any one of **three** ways in the Nominative:

-η   -α   -ης

Every first declension noun ends in one of these three ways. Now these endings are different enough to call for different endings in the rest of the cases (only in the singular, though). So we have to learn three different sets of endings for the first declension singular nouns. Fortunately the plural endings are all the same for all three groups.

Here are the three variations of first declension nouns. I used a sample noun with each variation to show how they would be declined.

ζωή; stem = ζω-

σκοτία; stem = σκοτί-

προφήτης; stem = προφήτ-

	Variation 1	Variation 2	Variation 3
Singular:			
Nom.:	ζωή	σκοτία	προφήτης
Gen.:	ζωῆς	σκοτίας	προφήτου
Dat.:	ζωῇ	σκοτίᾳ	προφήτῃ
Acc.:	ζωήν	σκοτίαν	προφήτην
Plural:			
Nom.:	ζωαί	σκοτίαι	προφήται
Gen.:	ζωῶν	σκοτίων	προφητῶν
Dat.:	ζωαῖς	σκοτίαις	προφήταις
Acc.:	ζωάς	σκοτίας	προφήτας

(Remember, the Greeks didn't just sit down and invent a difficult way of speaking their language. They didn't say, "Now we'll make this rule and that rule in order to make things complicated." Actually, they were speaking their language already when someone sat down to write a grammar for it. And all he did was to group together the common words that had the same characteristics. So all a grammar is, is someone describing to us how a certain people talked. Here it just so happened that these feminine nouns used these three endings – they're just what people always used. So we make a declension paradigm for each type and say, "Now whatever first declension word I find, I'll just put it in one of these three groups to help me remember it.")

Again, the stem is found by knocking off the Genitive ending from the dictionary form. Now don't get confused on how to use the stem; it's really very simple. When we get into some of the other cases and wonder where the root leaves off and the ending begins, there is where knowing the stem will be most useful. It tells you the exact dividing line between the word and its ending. Usually the word declines rather smoothly and you don't have to worry about the stem; but some words are tricky and we need some way to keep it orderly.

Vocabulary

Nouns

ἀγάπη, -ης, f.	love
ἀδελφή, -ῆς, f.	sister
ἀλήθεια, -ας, f.	truth
ἀρχή, -ῆς, f.	beginning
δόξα, -ας, f.	glory
ἐκκλησία, -ας, f.	church
ζωή, -ῆς, f.	life
μαθητής, -οῦ, m.	disciple
μαρτυρία, -ας, f.	witness
προφήτης, -ου, m.	prophet
σκοτία, -ας, f.	darkness
τιμή, -ῆς, f.	honor
τέκνον, -ου, n.	child
ὥρα, -ας, f.	hour

Verbs

βλέπει	he, she, or it sees
βλέπουσιν	they see

Other words

οὐκ	not
δέ	but

The verb "to be"

present		past		future	
εἰμί	ἐσμέν	ἤμην	ἦμεν	ἔσομαι	ἐσόμεθα
εἶ	ἐστέ	ἦς	ἦτε	ἔση	ἔσεσθε
ἐστίν	εἰσίν	ἦν	ἦσαν	ἔσται	ἔσονται

present		past		future	
I am	we are	I was	we were	I will be	we will be
you are	you are	you were	you were	you will be	you will be
he, she, it is	they are	he, she it was	they were	he, she, it will be	they will be

You will find exercises for this lesson on page: 109

SECOND CLASS WORDS – VERBS

So far we've studied all sorts of first class words – two declensions of nouns. They all have something in common: they all name and describe something.

Now we're going to go to another kind of word, one that does a different job in the sentence: the **verb**. The function that a verb has in a sentence is to tell us what action is going on. It tells us what the subject is doing or being or receiving from something else. It tells us whether the subject is actively doing something or just passively sitting under another's actions. It tells us when this action occurs. A verb, then, has to tell us a good deal about what's going on.

The Greek verb can do all this for us simply by adding certain letters onto the stem of the verb. In order to see what a verb can do for us, let's take an example to work on – the verb λύω, to "loose" (like *to loose* a boat from its anchor).

Present tense

Here's a paradigm of the verb λύω and its endings:

Person	Singular	Plural
1	λύω – I loose	λύομεν – we loose
2	λύεις – you (sing.) loose	λύετε – you (pl.) loose
3	λύει – he, she, it looses	λύουσιν – they loose

The endings are underlined, and by now you've probably figured out what they represent. They tell us the **number** (singular or plural) and the **person**. Person is who is doing the action – either the speaker (first person) or the person that the speaker is talking to (second person) or the person that the speaker is talking about (third person).

(In order to add the endings, you have to find the stem of the verb; and in order to find the stem of any verb that ends in **-ω**, simply knock off the **-ω** from the first person singular form and there's your stem!)

The verb will always tell us the person. Actually you usually have two subjects in a Greek sentence – the noun which acts as the subject, and the person of the verb. But you can leave the noun out and the verb will still tell you the person; you'll still have a complete sentence of verb and subject. For example,

$$\Theta\epsilon\acute{o}\varsigma\ \lambda\acute{u}\epsilon\iota\ \mathring{\alpha}\nu\theta\rho\omega\pi o\nu$$

Literally, this sentence reads "God, he looses a man." The pronoun "he" is built into the verb ending. In this sentence,

$$\lambda\acute{u}\epsilon\iota\ \mathring{\alpha}\nu\theta\rho\omega\pi o\nu$$

we would translate it, "He looses a man." You see, the subject is still there, even if we don't have a noun. English verbs don't work like that; without proper subjects we would be lost. But Greek verbs always tell us the person; the pronoun that's understood in the verb also has to match the gender, number, and person of the noun if there happens to be one.

There's another thing that verb endings tell us – the *tense* of the verb. Tense is *when* the action happened; and basically there are three kinds of tenses:

present
past
future

Different tenses have different endings; the ones that you've just learned are the present tense endings. That means that the action is happening at the same time that the speaker is talking about it.

By the way, putting the verb into this kind of paradigm is called ***conjugating*** the verb, and the arrangement of a verb with its endings is called a ***conjugation***. The idea is exactly like the declension of nouns. There's good news, though: there's only one conjugation (unlike the nouns, with *three* declensions!). If we were studying Latin you would have four of them! But in Greek, every regular present tense verb uses these particular endings – always.

Future tense

We should look at the future tense endings while we're at it, because it's the easiest thing in the world to change a verb from present to future. This is how: simply take the stem of the verb, stick on a sigma (**σ**), and then use the present tense endings. That makes a future tense verb. Here is the verb λύω conjugated in the future tense:

Person	Singular	Plural
1	λύσ<u>ω</u> – I will loose	λύσ<u>ομεν</u> – we will loose
2	λύσ<u>εις</u> – you (sing.) will loose	λύσ<u>ετε</u> – you (pl.) will loose
3	λύσ<u>ει</u> – he, she, it will loose	λύσ<u>ουσιν</u> – they will loose

Future tense means that the action is yet to happen from the time the speaker is talking. Future verbs also tell us the three important facts:

person

number

tense

And future verbs are really built from present tense verbs, because they use the same stem and the same endings.

Changing the stem

There's just one little problem with forming the future tense. Adding the sigma (**σ**) is all right for the verbs with stems that end in a vowel, like λύω. But many verbs have stems that end with a consonant, like βλέπω. Its stem is βλεπ-, ending in **π**. What would we have if we added the sigma for the future tense?

βλέπσω

That sound ought to ring a bell. The combination **πσ** is already represented in the Greek letter psi (**ψ**). So why not write a **ψ** when we're forming the future, like this:

βλέψω

It's a lot simpler to do that. As a matter of fact, when you add a **σ** onto any consonant it either makes it sound like another letter or it gets shortened down.

Here's a chart showing what new letters appear when you add a σ onto the consonants.

To the consonant:	Add:	and you get:

To the consonant:	Add:	and you get:
π	σ	ψ
β	σ	ψ
φ	σ	ψ
πτ	σ	ψ

κ	σ	ξ
γ	σ	ξ
χ	σ	ξ
σσ	σ	ξ

δ	σ	σ
θ	σ	σ
ζ	σ	σ

Vocabulary

Verbs

ἄγω	I lead
βαπτίζω	I baptize
γράφω	I write
διώκω	I persecute
λύω	I loose
πείθω	I persuade
πέμπω	I send

Nouns

βασιλεία, -ας, f.	kingdom
ἔργον, -ου, n.	work
ὄχλος, -ου, m.	crowd
υἱός, -οῦ, m.	son

Other words

καθώς	as
οὖν	therefore
τότε	then

You will find exercises for this lesson on page: 115

OTHER FIRST CLASS WORDS:
PRONOUNS, ADJECTIVES, ARTICLES

By now you ought to be used to declensions and endings. In this lesson we'll look at three other kinds of first class words – the pronoun, the adjective, and the article – all of which you can decline exactly the way you declined the nouns. As a matter of fact, you won't even need to learn any new declensions, because all three of these use the first and second declensions.

Pronouns

A pronoun identifies something, or names it, just like a noun does. It stands in the place of a noun and names in a general way what the noun identifies more specifically. And, just like a noun, a pronoun has gender, number, and case endings.

Suppose we have a sentence like this:

She caught the ball.

"She" is the pronoun; it stands in the place of some noun that we already know about (perhaps "the girl") and plays the role of subject in the sentence. A pronoun can play any role that a noun has – subject, object, possessive, or indirect object.

Greek pronouns are the same way. And since they can stand in the place of a noun, they can be put into a declension. But since a pronoun can take the place of feminine as well as masculine nouns, the pronoun paradigm must have all three genders. Here is the full paradigm for Greek pronouns:

Singular:

	he (masculine)	she (feminine)	it (neuter)
Nom.:	αὐτός	αὐτή	αὐτό
Gen.:	αὐτοῦ	αὐτῆς	αὐτοῦ
Dat.:	αὐτῷ	αὐτῇ	αὐτῷ
Acc.:	αὐτόν	αὐτήν	αὐτό

Plural:

	they (masculine)	they (feminine)	they (neuter)
Nom.:	αὐτοί	αὐταί	αὐτά
Gen.:	αὐτῶν	αὐτῶν	αὐτῶν
Dat.:	αὐτοῖς	αὐταῖς	αὐτοῖς
Acc.:	αὐτούς	αὐτάς	αὐτά

The stem – αὐτ – actually means "self"; so these are personal pronouns because they refer to the persons themselves. This same stem forms the root of our English words "automobile" (moves by itself), and "autobiography" (a life story written by oneself).

So if you have the stem, you can easily decline the whole paradigm of the personal pronoun. "He" uses the second declension endings (naturally – since they're masculine endings), "she" uses the first declension feminine endings, and "it" uses the second declension neuter endings.

Adjectives

Adjectives identify something by describing it: big or little, hot or cold, white or black, and so on. But adjectives, since they describe things, always have to be associated with some noun or pronoun; you'll never find a stray adjective. The noun or pronoun that it describes has to be somewhere near in the sentence.

It stands to reason, then, that the adjective must have the same gender, number, and case that its noun or pronoun has. So the same rule holds as for the personal pronoun: since an adjective must have all the same characteristics of any noun, it must be declinable.

(Just for future reference, I'm going to throw a wrench in the works here. An adjective doesn't have to use the same **declension** as its noun or pronoun. There's another declension in Greek; some nouns belong to this third declension and so do some adjectives. So if one of the adjectives that you're learning now happens to describe a third declension noun in a sentence, it still must use its own **first** or **second** declension endings, since it's not a third declension adjective [you'll learn those later]. Therefore we have to talk about adjective endings not as declension endings but as *gender* endings; an adjective will always have the same gender as its noun.)

Now think a minute – if an adjective can describe a noun, it must be able to do triple duty. It has to be able to describe masculine and feminine and neuter nouns; so it has to have a choice of endings of all three genders. Here's a complete paradigm of a single adjective:

καλός – good; stem = καλ-

Singular:

	masculine	feminine	neuter
Nom.:	καλός	καλή	καλόν
Gen.:	καλοῦ	καλῆς	καλοῦ
Dat.:	καλῷ	καλῇ	καλῷ
Acc.:	καλόν	καλήν	καλόν

Plural:

Nom.:	καλοί	καλαί	καλά
Gen.:	καλῶν	καλῶν	καλῶν
Dat.:	καλοῖς	καλαῖς	καλοῖς
Acc.:	καλούς	καλάς	καλά

Attributive or predicate?

Adjectives can do one of two things in the sentence: they either stand beside a noun and qualify it, or stand on the other side of a verb and qualify the subject. One is an *attributive* adjective, and the other is a *predicate* adjective. For example, in the phrase –

the good boy

"good" is an attributive adjective. It tells us about some attribute that the boy has. But in the sentence –

The boy is good.

"good is a predicate adjective; it follows the verb "is" which acts just like an equals sign (if you remember your English grammar you'll know what "predicate" means). Of course, it makes no difference which type the adjective is; it still agrees with its noun's gender, number, and person. But you need to know when the adjective is predicate so that you can translate it correctly.

To summarize, a predicate adjective will either –

- follow an equative verb ("is", "are", etc.)

- be missing an article of its own, even though its noun has one. For example,

καλός ὁ Θεός – "Good is God" (literally) – and
ὁ Θεός καλός – "God is good" – are both **predicate**; but …

ὁ καλός Θεός – "the good God" – and
ὁ Θεός ὁ καλός – "the good God" – are both **attributive**.

What if there is no article, neither on the noun or adjective? Then it could be either predicate or attributive! You'll have to judge that for yourself by studying the context.

Articles

An article is really a form of adjective. It describes a noun or pronoun by pointing at it, singling it out from a crowd, so to speak. It emphasizes that word: *the* book, not just any book.

In English we have three articles: *a*, *an*, and *the*. But in Greek there's only one: *the*.

Since an article is like an adjective, it has the same grammatical characteristics as an adjective: it has to have the same gender, case, and number as the noun it's connected to. And it also has to do triple duty, because it must be able to describe masculine, feminine, or neuter nouns.

Following is the complete paradigm for the article:

Singular:

	masculine	feminine	neuter
Nom.:	ὁ	ἡ	τό
Gen.:	τοῦ	τῆς	τοῦ
Dat.:	τῷ	τῇ	τῷ
Acc.:	τόν	τήν	τόν

<u>Plural</u>:

Nom.:	οἱ	αἱ	τά
Gen.:	τῶν	τῶν	τῶν
Dat.:	τοῖς	ταῖς	τοῖς
Acc.:	τούς	τάς	τά

The Greek article is always translated "the". But it isn't always necessary to translate it. It emphasizes its noun by bringing attention to it; but sometimes it would be awkward to translate it. For example, Θεός often has an article, but we would hardly want to translate it as "the God"!

The article plays an extremely important role in addition to emphasizing a noun – it tells what gender the noun is. We've already learned these words:

προφήτης and μαθητής

We could get mixed up by their endings and think that they're feminine gender, since they are first declension nouns. But you'll **always** find these –

ὁ προφήτης and ὁ μαθητής

You will **never** see these:

ἡ προφήτης and ἡ μαθητής

The article tells us that they are masculine nouns. You're never in the dark about a noun's gender if it has an article with it.

So from now on, the dictionary form of the noun will have the article that goes with that noun, instead of the gender abbreviation, like this:

Θεός, -οῦ, ὁ   God

Vocabulary

Adjectives

ἅγιος, α, ον	holy
δίκαιος, α, ον	righteous
ἴδιος, α, ον	one's own
καλός, ή, όν	good
μακάριος, α, ον	blessed, happy
μικρός, ά, όν	small
νεκρός, ά, όν	dead
πονηρός, ά, όν	sinful, wicked
πρεσβύτερος, α, ον	older, elder

(**Note:** in the dictionary, adjectives will be listed like this, showing the Nominative singular endings for masculine, feminine, and neuter, to help you decline them correctly.)

Nouns

ἄγγελος, -ου, ὁ	angel
ἀδελφός, -οῦ, ὁ	brother
ἁμαρτία, -ας, ἡ	sin
ἡμέρα, -ας, ἡ	day
καρδία, -ας, ἡ	heart

κύριος, -ου, ὁ	Lord
οὐρανός, -οῦ, ὁ	heaven

Verbs

ἀκολουθέω	I follow
ἀποκτείνω (future, ἀποκ‑ενῶ)	I kill

Other words

γάρ	for
ὡς	that
ἤ	or

You will find exercises for this lesson on page: 121

SECOND CLASS WORDS – VERBS, PAST TENSE

Two kinds of past action

The Greeks had two kinds of past tense. They needed two because past tense isn't as simple as talking about things that already happened. It could have been an on-going action or an action that was started and completed. So they made two different past tenses to cover both these possibilities.

For example, in the sentence –

The boy was running.

"was running" is a past tense verb. It tells what the boy was doing in the past in reference to the speaker's present time. But notice that it's an on-going action; he was in the *process* of running. We're not told when he stopped running, or even if he did stop; he could very well *still* be running for all we know. This kind of past tense is called the ***imperfect*** tense – because the action hasn't been "perfected" or completed as far as we know.

But if we say –

The boy was running and the dog bit him.

"bit" is a different kind of past tense. It tells about what the dog did in a way that we can know more about *when* it happened. There was a time when the dog bit the boy, and it finished or "completed" the action. "Was running", however, is a process, and therefore imperfect; but "bit" was a definite action completed *within* the story. This tense is called the ***aorist*** tense in Greek.

As you can see, the way we translate the Greek imperfect tense verb is usually by adding "ing" to the end of the verb's translation, and also by using a "helper" verb out front – like this: ***was*** runn***ing***. Aorist tense is usually translated simply by adding the letters "ed" on the end of the verb's translation.

Forming past tenses

How do we make these tenses in Greek? Since they are two different tenses, they naturally have two different sets of endings. But they both share a characteristic: to form both of them, you have to add an epsilon (ϵ) on the beginning of the stem. So for the past tenses we have to add special letters on the beginning *and* the end of the stem. Here are the steps to form both tenses:

Imperfect:

	singular		plural
ϵ-	-oν (I was -ing)	ϵ-	-oμϵν (we were -ing)
ϵ-	-ϵς (you were -ing)	ϵ-	-ϵτϵ (you were -ing)
ϵ-	-ϵν (he, she, it was -ing)	ϵ-	-oν (they were -ing)

Aorist:

	singular		plural
ϵ-	-σα (I -ed)	ϵ-	-σαμϵν (we -ed)
ϵ-	-σας (you -ed)	ϵ-	-σατϵ (you -ed)
ϵ-	-σϵν (he, she, it -ed)	ϵ-	-σαν (they -ed)

Now let's take an example. Here's the verb λύω in the imperfect and the aorist tenses; follow it through and see what happens to it:

Imperfect:

singular	plural
ἔλυον (I was loosing)	ἐλύομϵν
ἔλυϵς	ἐλύϵτϵ
ἔλυϵν	ἔλυον

Aorist:

singular	plural
ἔλυσα (I loosed)	ἐλύσαμεν
ἔλυσας	ἐλύσατε
ἔλυσεν	ἔλυσαν

The verb stem is underlined so that you can see what was stuck on it at either end. As a matter of fact, it ought to be easy to see that it's just a matter of what letters get stuck onto either side of the basic verb stem. Remember that and you'll never have any problem with past tenses.

Maybe a little memory device will help here. Think of a verb as someone's head. The stem is the head itself, and the letters stuck onto the stem are the ears on either side of the head. Just take a hold of the verb's ears and shake it good: "Who are you? And tell me what kind of ears you have!"

Now, sometimes a verb stem doesn't start out with a consonant – it may start with a vowel. In that case, adding an ε onto the beginning of a word stem that starts with a vowel will change that vowel into some other letter. In other words, the vowel of the verb plus the ε will turn both into a new vowel.

Here's an example: say you want to make the verb ἀκούω in the imperfect tense, first person singular. First put the "ears" on:

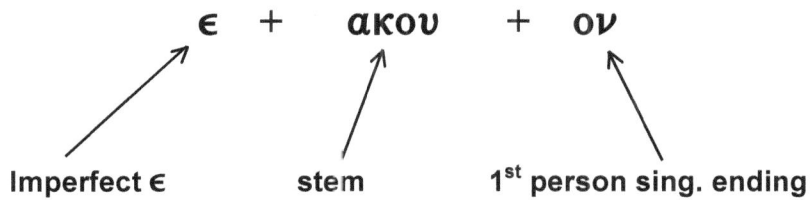

$$\epsilon \quad + \quad \alpha\kappa o \upsilon \quad + \quad o\nu$$

Imperfect ε   stem   1st person sing. ending

But adding an **ε** with an **α** looks funny, and it's a little tough to pronounce:

$$\epsilon\breve{\alpha}\kappa o\upsilon o\nu$$

So let's change the **εα** into an **η**, like this:

$$\mathring{\eta}\kappa o\upsilon o\nu$$

Now we have the finished product.

Here's a chart to help you decide what to change a vowel into when you have to add an **ε** for the past tenses:

When the stem starts with:	and you're adding:	change both into:
α	ε	η
ε	ε	η
ο	ε	ω
ι	ε	ι
υ	ε	υ
αι	ε	η
αυ	ε	ηυ
οι	ε	ω
ευ	ε	ηυ

Just one more thing to notice: when making the aorist, you add a σ onto the stem, right? Well, if the stem happens to end in a consonant like ϕ or γ or β, adding the σ next to these letters will suddenly change both letters into a new single letter, just like we saw in the lesson on future verbs. Just use the chart there (page 39) for changing these aorist verbs too.

Vocabulary

Verbs

αἴρω   I take

Future 3 p.s. ἀρεῖ
Aorist – ἦρα
Imperfect – ἦρον

ἐλπίζω   I hope

Future – ἐλπιῶ
Aorist – ἤλπισα
Imperfect – ἤλπιζον

ἐσθίω   I eat

ἔχω   I have

καλύπτω   I hide

κελεύω   I command

κηρύσσω   I preach

ὀφείλω   I owe

πείθω   I persuade

Aorist – ἔπεισα
Imperfect – ἔπειθεν
Future – πείσω

ὑποστρέφω   I return

(**Note**: Sometimes a verb isn't regularly formed in all of the tenses; and when you look for it in the lexicon, it will tell you how to form it in the troublesome tenses. If it doesn't mention any possible problems, then that verb is regularly formed – that is, you just follow the normal rules.)

Nouns

ἄρτος, -ου, ὁ	bread
εἰρήνη, -ης, ἡ	peace
θάλασσα, -ης, ἡ	sea, lake
οἰκία, -ας, ἡ	house
ὀφθαλμός, -οῦ, ὁ	eye
πλοῖον, -ου, τό	a boat

Pronouns

ἐγώ	I

Adjectives

ἄλλος, η, ο	other
ἔσχατος, η, ον	last
ἱκανός, ή, όν	sufficient
κακός, ή, όν	bad
πιστός, ή, όν	faithful

You will find exercises for this lesson on page: 127

THIRD CLASS WORDS

So far we've studied a lot about first class and second class words, and how they're used in sentences. Now we'll look at the last class, or type, of words – the third class. Here we have everything that didn't fall into the first or second classes: *adverbs, prepositions, negatives,* and *conjunctions.* All of them share one characteristic: they don't decline or conjugate or fit into any paradigm. You just use them as they are.

Adverbs

Adverbs are words that describe. Remember that adjectives describe nouns and pronouns. Well, adverbs describe the other parts of speech – verbs, adjectives, and other adverbs. For example, in the sentence "He walked lazily," the word "lazily" is an adverb that describes *how* he walked. Usually you can say that the adverb tells us **how**, **when, where**, or **how much** whenever it describes a word.

Most adverbs are easy to spot in Greek because they usually end in **-ως**. Here are some Greek adverbs:

ἀγνῶς	purely
ἀληθῶς	truly
ὄντως	really
ὑπερβαλλόντως	exceedingly

While most adverbs end in **-ως**, there are many others that don't; their endings are usually one of the following:

-οτε,	like	τότε	then
-θεν,	like	μακρόθεν	from afar
-ω,	like	οὔπω	not yet
-ου,	like	ὅπου	where
-ις,	like	μόλις	hardly

And then there are other adverbs that don't end in any particular way, like these:

ἀμήν	truly
ἐκεῖ	there
λίαν	very
ναί	yes

Prepositions

Let's look a little at the grammar of the preposition now.

Every preposition takes a noun or a pronoun for its object (and sometimes a participle). The object of a preposition has to be of a certain case (remember, in Greek a noun has to have a case ending, wherever it is in the sentence!). Which case ending it has depends on what the preposition prefers. Some prepositions like certain cases and not other cases. Some prepositions like all the cases, but attach a certain meaning to each case. For example, let's look at the preposition **παρά**:

> **When the object is in the GENITIVE case,**   **παρά means FROM**
>
> **When the object is in the DATIVE case,**   **παρά means WITH**
>
> **When the object is in the ACCUSATIVE case,**   **παρά means BESIDE**

For example, you would use it like this:

> παρά του Θεου – from God
>
> παρά τη αληθεια – with the truth
>
> παρά τόν τεκνον – beside the child

Your lexicon will tell you how to translate a preposition. Just remember that it will ask you what case its object is in – that makes a difference as to what its meaning will be.

Negatives

Negatives fall into two types: the kind that's used with indicative (that is, the type we've learned so far) verbs, and the kind that's used with other moods of verbs. The negatives that are used the most are **οὐ** and **μή**. They both mean **no** or **not**.

For indicative verbs you use **οὐ** to express the idea of **no** – whether present or future action. Of course, **οὐ** can be used anywhere in the sentence, not just with a verb. But if the mood of the whole sentence is indicative then you'll find **οὐ**.

For the other moods – subjunctive, imperative, participle, infinitive – **μή** is used instead. This is a handy way, you might have noticed, to tell what mood the verb is in (in case you can't remember its special endings!). **μή** is never used with indicative verbs.

A lot of negatives are built up from these two basic words. Here are a few of them and their meanings.

οὐ	μή	Meaning
οὐδείς	μηδείς	no one
οὔπω	μήπω	not yet
οὐδέπω	μηδέπω	not yet
οὐθείς	μηθείς	no one
οὐκ		no, not
οὐκι		no, not

Conjunctions

You've been using conjunctions all along now, but it's time we looked at them too. Conjunctions are words that *connect*. A conjunction connects one section of a sentence with another section. It can connect two small sentences together, or a phrase and a sentence, or two phrases, to make one bigger sentence. Conjunctions even connect single words together.

Here are some much-used conjunctions:

καί	and	(καί … καί – and … and) *
τέ	and	(τέ … τέ – both … and)
ἤ	or	(ἤ … ἤ – either … or)
ἀλλά	but	(οὐ μόνον … ἀλλά καί – not only … but also)
οὔτε	nor	(οὔτε … οὔτε – neither … nor)
γάρ	for	
δέ	but, and	
οὖν	so, then	
ἄρα	then	

(* **Note:** The single word is translated "and"; but if you find two of them separated by a few other words in a sentence, then you translate the first one "and" and the second one "and". The same pattern goes for the following conjunctions as well.)

We should look at another kind of conjunction – the type that starts off a clause inside a larger sentence. For example, in the sentence "I hope that you are faithful," the phrase "I hope" is the main sentence with subject and verb. But "you are faithful" is a little sentence inside the whole idea; it's called the *subordinate clause*. The conjunction "that" is the clue that there's a subordinate clause following next; so it's called the *subordinating conjunction*. Big name for a little word! They are important, though. Here are some of the more common subordinating conjunctions:

διότι	because, for
ἐπεί	since, because
ἔως	until, while
καθώς	as
ὅτι	that, because
ὡς	as
ὥσπερ	as
ὥστε	so that

Vocabulary

Adverbs

ἀληθώς	truly
ἀμήν	truly
ἄνωθεν	from above
ἄρτι	now
ἐκεῖ	there
νῦν	now
ὄντως	really
οὐδέποτε	never
ὅπου	where
οὔπω	not yet
πάλιν	again
πάντοτε	always
πρῶτον	first

Negatives

μή	no, not
οὐ, οὐκ	no, not

Conjunctions

ἀλλά	but
ἆρα	then
γάρ	for
δέ	but, and
ἤ	or
και	and
οὖν	so, then
οὔτε	nor
τέ	and

Prepositions

διά	through
ἐν	in
παρά	for, with, beside
προς	to, for

Nouns

ἀνήρ, ἀνδρός, ὁ	man
βιβλίον, -ου, τό	book
γραμματεύς, -έως, ὁ	scribe

συναγωγή, -ῆς, ἡ	synagogue

Verbs

εὐχαριστέω	I give thanks
θέλω	I wish
μετανοέω	I repent

You will find exercises for this lesson on page: 133

INTERLUDE

Before we go on, perhaps a word or two is needed to make a few points plain.

These lessons teach you Greek from a certain point of view: that is, how to *construct* a particular word with its endings. This helps you do your homework, because you are asked to create new Greek words according to the rules you have learned. But in another sense, it isn't really the way you'll be approaching the Greek New Testament. Once you've learned Greek, your constructing days will be over, so to speak. From then on you will study the Bible – and that's already written, fixed, unchanging.

So you have to get into a new frame of mind when you're translating the text. What I mean is this: when you are studying a word, you have to know **how the word got that way**; in other words, *why* does it have these particular endings? Now instead of making a new word, you'll be reasoning backwards to find out the history of a word – what the endings are, and what the stem must therefore be.

For example, let's take a word and analyze it. In John 1:14 is the following word:

$$\text{ἐσκήνωσεν}$$

Let's attack it scientifically. First, look up the word in the lexicon – but it isn't there. The beginning letters ἐσκη- don't appear in any words there. That's a clue that the leading ϵ must have been added onto the stem. And that means that the stem must be something close to σκην-.

Next, since the ending looks suspiciously like a verb ending, check the ending against the verb chart (you'll find it later in this book on page 90). The letters **-σεν** match the aorist indicative, third person singular form. So the word is in past tense, and it's a verb (now we know it's not a noun!).

Next, look up σκην- in the dictionary. The word σκηνόω is there – it means "to live, dwell."

Now we can explain how the stem melted into the ending: the stem σκηνο- merges with **-οσεν** to form σκηνοοσεν, and the aorist leading ϵ gets stuck onto the beginning: ἐσκήνοοσεν. But since two omicrons won't ever sit next to each other, they merge to form an **ω**: ἐσκήνωσεν.

Now we can translate the word: *he lived*.

There's nothing hard about that. You just have to keep your cool and walk through the steps. Don't be ashamed about using other helps like this; nobody but a bona-fide Greek scholar can read anywhere in the text without helps! The point is to track down the grammar, to gradually unpack the word until you know exactly what the stem was and how all the endings and prefixes got stuck on.

SECOND CLASS WORDS – MIDDLE AND PASSIVE

Action is always headed somewhere. When someone does something, he does it *out to* an object – like a boy throwing a ball. He impels energy to the ball and makes it do what he wants.

But direction can go two ways. For instance, the action could be coming back to the person himself – he may be the object of someone else's action. In this case, we say that the action is directed *toward oneself*, instead of away from oneself.

So far the verb forms that we've studied were in the ***active voice*** – which means action directed *out from* the subject *toward* another object. There are two other voices, both in English and in Greek: the ***middle voice***, and the ***passive voice***.

Middle voice describes an action that the subject does *to himself*. For example: The elephant *washed itself*. The problem about the middle voice is that its meaning is sometimes uncertain. Though you can generally translate it as action done to oneself, it doesn't always mean that. You'll have to check the dictionary to get the correct meaning.

Passive voice describes an action that another person does *to the subject*. For example: The elephant *was washed* by the zookeeper.

Following are the middle and passive voices of the verb λύω.

Middle voice:

singular	plural
λυομαι (I loose myself)	λυόμεθα
λυη	λύεσθε
λυεται	λύονται

Passive voice:

singular	plural
λυομαι (I am loosed, or set loose)	λυόμεθα
λυη	λύεσθε
λυεται	λύονται

Notice that the middle and passive voices for λύω are the same. This isn't always the case, though, for other verbs. You'll have to check the dictionary when you look up a verb to see if the passive voice has different forms from the middle voice.

(**Note:** some Greek verbs are irregularly formed. When the verb has an active meaning, it may have a middle form. For example, γίνωμαι means "to become" (an active meaning), but it has the middle form – it has no active forms in the present tense. You'll just have to watch out for these and learn them.)

There are also past tense forms for the middle and passive voices. For the verb λύω, it would mean "I was loosed" or "I loosed myself." You can see these past tense forms on the verb chart on page 90.

Vocabulary

Nouns

ἀγρός, -οῦ, ὁ	a field
διδάσκαλος, -ου, ὁ	teacher
δῶρον, -ου, τό	a gift
θάνατος, -ου, ὁ	death
ἱερόν, -οῦ, τό	a temple
λίθος, -ου, ὁ	a stone
χαρά, -ᾶς, ἡ	joy

Adjectives

ἁμαρτωλός, ή, ού	sinful
Ἰουδαῖος, α, ον	Jewish

Verbs

ἐγείρω	I raise up
κρίνω	I judge
πειράζω	I tempt
χαίρω	I rejoice

Personal pronouns

ἐγώ	I	ἡμεῖς	we
ἐμοῦ, μου	of me	ἡμῶν	of us
ἐμοί, μοι	to, for me	ἡμῖν	to, for us
ἐμέ, με	me	ἡμᾶς	us
σύ	you	ὑμεῖς	you all
σοῦ	of you	ὑμῶν	of you all
σοί	to, for you	ὑμῖν	to, for you all
σέ	you	ὑμᾶς	you all

(**Note:** Remember that the Greek pronouns for *he, she, it,* and *they* are αὐτός, αὐτή, αὐτό, and the plural forms of these words.)

You will find exercises for this lesson on page: 139

FIRST CLASS WORDS – THIRD DECLENSION
THIRD CLASS WORDS – PREPOSITIONS

Need for another declension

There are a lot of other nouns in *koine* Greek that don't have first or second declension endings; these form a third declension with a special set of endings all their own.

At first sight we would tend to think that any noun that didn't fit into the other declensions must have been thrown into this "catch all" declension, because we seem to have all kinds of strange endings for these nouns. The Nominative singular endings for the first declension nouns were either **-η, -ης,** or **-α.** The second declension nouns all end in **-ος** (for masculine) and **-ον** (for neuter). But the third declension nouns have Nominative endings like **-ξ, -ς, -α, -ν, -ρ, -υς, -ις, -ους, -ος,** and various other ways!

But we're not going to worry about all that. We're just going to learn two things: **first**, the dictionary form for the third declension nouns, and **second**, the third declension endings. We'll find that there's really no problem after all about so many different endings.

Dictionary form

In the dictionary, a third declension noun will look like this:

σάρξ,   σαρκός,   ἡ   flesh

1   2   3   4

1 – the Nominative singular form of the word

2 – the Genitive singular form. This tells us that it's a third declension noun, because the third declension ending for the Genitive case is *always* **-ος**.

3 – the article telling us the gender of the noun – in this case, feminine.

4 - the meaning of the word.

Here's another word:

$$πνεῦμα, -ματος, τό \qquad\qquad \text{spirit}$$

Notice that the Genitive ending only is given here, since the stem is easy to figure out. Only if the stem can't be easily figured out from the Nominative form will the full Genitive spelling be given.

Third declension paradigm

Following are the paradigms for both of these third declension nouns. Notice that it makes no difference how the Nominative singular is spelled; we start with the Genitive form to come up with the rest. (Remember the advice I gave you before about getting the stem of the noun from the Genitive form? Well, here's why! Third declension Nominative forms are so undependable for finding the stem.)

$$σάρξ, \quad σαρκός, \quad ἡ \qquad \text{flesh}$$

	singular	plural
Nom.:	ἡ σάρξ	αἱ σαρκές
Gen.:	της σαρκός	των σαρκῶν
Dat.:	τη σαρκί	ταις σαρξίν *
Acc.:	την σαρκά	τας σαρκάς

$$πνεῦμα, -ματος, τό \qquad\qquad \text{spirit}$$

	singular	plural
Nom.:	τό πνεῦμα	τά πνεύματα
Gen.:	τοῦ πνευμᾶτος	τῶν πνευμάτων
Dat.:	τῷ πνεύματι	τοῖς πνεύμασιν
Acc.:	τό πνεῦμα	τά πνεύματα

(*** Note:** The dative plural is really **-σιν**. So when you add it to the stem of a noun, you may have to change the last letter of the stem. As we saw in the lesson on future verbs, when you combine a **σ** with another consonant, you end up with a new consonant. So here, the stem σαρκ- takes the ending **-σιν**, and the **κσ** combination turns into **ξ**.)

Combined with adjectives

A little reminder here: now that you have new nouns to memorize – and they're all third declension – don't lose your cool when you find them combined with adjectives carrying a first or second declension ending. Adjectives use endings to show **gender**, not declension. So an adjective with a second declension ending is really reflecting the **masculine** gender of the noun that it's describing. It's perfectly all right for the two words – adjective and noun – to have different endings as long as this rule is kept in mind.

For example, here is a **first** declension adjective (and the article!) that describes a **third** declension noun:

ἡ καλή μήτηρ

A preposition chart

We need to get introduced to prepositions, because we can't do much translation work without them. We've already looked at some of the important grammatical uses of prepositions; but now you should at least get familiar with some more of them.

Following is a chart of prepositions. In the middle is a circle, and surrounding it are lines going different directions in respect to the circle. Each line represents a preposition; beside the preposition is its meaning. The meaning tells us what the line is doing in respect to the circle itself. For example, the line with ἐν (in) is **inside** the circle. The ἀνά (up) line is moving **up** from the circle. διά (through) is moving **through** the circle. So you can get from this chart a visual idea of the basic meaning of the preposition.

If you know anything about grammar you know that a preposition needs an object. The object of the preposition is either a noun or a pronoun, so it can be declined in a paradigm. So, what case must the noun or pronoun be in when it's attached to a preposition? Well, beside each prepositional meaning on the chart is the case that the object of that preposition must be in. For example, ἐν demands the Dative case; thus we read "in Christ" – ἐν Χριστῷ. Χριστῷ is in the Dative case.

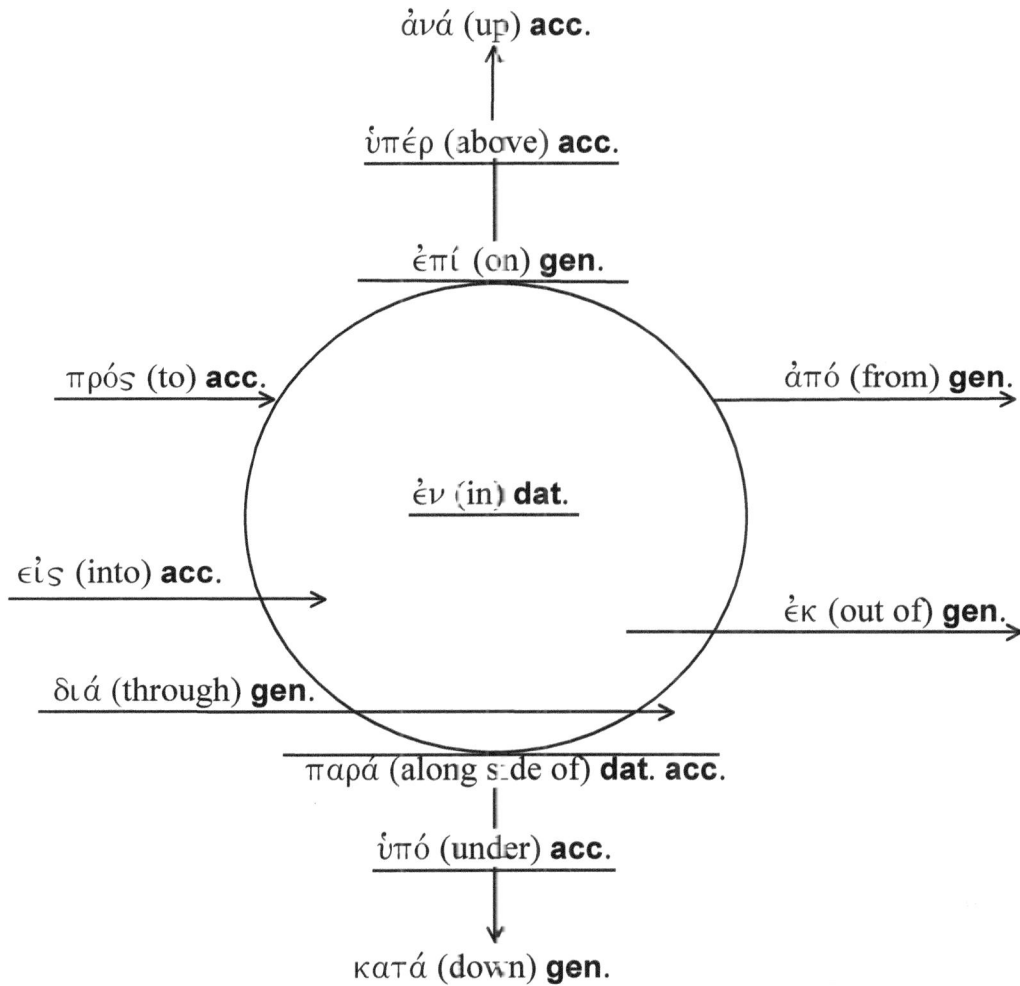

ἀνά (up) **acc.**

ὑπέρ (above) **acc.**

ἐπί (on) **gen.**

πρός (to) **acc.**

ἀπό (from) **gen.**

ἐν (in) **dat.**

εἰς (into) **acc.**

ἐκ (out of) **gen.**

διά (through) **gen.**

παρά (along side of) **dat. acc.**

ὑπό (under) **acc.**

κατά (down) **gen.**

Vocabulary

Nouns

γυνή, γυναικός, ἡ	woman
δαίμων, -ονος, ὁ	demon
ἐλπίς, -ίδος, ἡ	hope
ἱμάτιον, -οῦ, τό	garment
ἰχθύς, -θύος, ὁ	fish
κώμη, -ης, ἡ	village
νύξ, νυκτός, ἡ	night
ὄνομα, ὀνόματος, τό	name
πατήρ, πατρός, ὁ	father
πνεῦμα, -τος, τό	spirit
σάρξ, σαρκός, ἡ	flesh
στρατιώτης, -ου, ὁ	soldier
σῶμα, -ματος, ἡ	body
σωτήρ, -ῆρος, ὁ	savior
ὕδωρ, ὕδατος, τό	water
φῶς, φωτός, τό	light
χάρις, χάριστος, ἡ	grace

Verbs

αἰτέω	I ask
πάσχω	I suffer
περιπατέω	I walk

You will find exercises for this lesson on page: 145

SECOND CLASS WORDS – SUBJUNCTIVE MOOD

Mood

Verbs have a characteristic called *mood*. It means exactly what you'd think it would mean – mood is what the speaker feels when he's describing some action. He might feel that the action is –

really happening – a fact ——————> indicative mood

might possibly happen ——————> subjunctive mood

it better happen! ——————> imperative mood

an undefined happening ——————> infinitive mood

a continuous happening ——————> participle mood

These are different ways of feeling about the action – different ways of speaking about it. In this lesson, we're going to look at the subjunctive mood.

Meaning of the subjunctive

The subjunctive mood is the wish-possibility mood. We wish something would happen, or there's a possibility that it might happen. In English we don't use the subjunctive much; but Greek uses it a lot. The subjunctive is used in commands, "if-then" clauses, and strong negatives about the future – like "may it never be!"

There's a lot of similarity between the subjunctive and the simple future indicative, which makes sense if you think about it. Future tense means that something *will* happen or is yet to happen; subjunctive mood means it *might* happen or we'd like it to happen. They both refer to an action not yet started: one speaks of it in a matter-of-fact way, and the other leaves some doubt that it might happen unless certain conditions are first met.

Subjunctive paradigms

The subjunctive has its own set of endings, as we'd expect. Only we don't have to worry about so many tenses in the subjunctive mood – there are only two: ***present*** and ***aorist***. (There's no future tense in subjunctive, because if you want to talk about something in the future tense then just use the simple future indicative instead.)

Here are the paradigms for the verb λύω in the subjunctive mood:

λύω, to loose. Stem = λυ-

person	present	aorist
Singular		
1	λύω (I might loose)	λύσω
2	λύῃς	λύσῃς
3	λύῃ	λύσῃ
Plural		
1	λύωμεν	λύσωμεν
2	λύητε	λύσητε
3	λύωσιν	λύσωσιν

It's easier than it looks. These endings are the same indicative endings that you learned with the present tense! The difference is that the vowel of the ending that follows the stem is lengthened (that is, ε becomes η; o becomes ω; ει becomes η; and ου becomes ω). That's the only difference. The aorist, of course, gets a sigma (σ) added onto the stem; and then it uses the same endings! So the subjunctive paradigms are actually very simple to learn.

Uses of the subjunctive

There are many ways that the subjunctive mood is used in a sentence. But usually it's found in dependent clauses. A ***dependent clause*** is a complete thought that's found within a larger sentence. For example, in the sentence –

God sent the disciple so that he might preach.

"so that he might preach" is a complete thought of its own, with its own subject, verb, and object. But it makes no sense by itself; its meaning is only clear inside the larger sentence structure.

"Sent" is a regular indicative mood verb; it's a straightforward action, future tense. But "might preach" has to be a subjunctive verb; it's talking about something that *might* happen, not necessarily what *will* happen. Do you see the element of possibility in this sentence? You need the subjunctive to do this job.

Dependent clauses happen frequently in the Greek Bible. There's almost always a clue word, though, that warns us of the presence of the subjunctive verb (how nice!). There are several clue words, but the most popular one is ἵνα. Whenever you see this word, you can be sure that there's a subjunctive following along behind. ἵνα means "in order that" or "so that", and it always starts off a dependent clause – like this:

Θεός ἐπέμψεν τόν μαθήτην ἵνα κηρύξῃ.

God sent the disciple so that he might preach.

The main verb of the sentence is ἐπέμψεν, which is an aorist indicative. ἵνα warns us of an up-coming subjunctive verb – which is κηρύξῃ, aorist subjunctive. (Note how the **σσ** of the stem gets changed to **ξ**; see the chart in the first lesson on verbs, on page 39.)

Other subjunctives that you'll meet in the Greek Bible will be used in many ways; but with your lexicon and grammar in hand, and remembering that the subjunctive is the wish or possibility mood, you won't have any trouble translating them.

Vocabulary

Verbs

ἀκούω	I hear
ἀνοίγω	I open
ἀποθνήσκω	I die
ἀποκρίνομαι	I answer
ἀποστέλλω	I send
διδάσκω	I teach
δύναμαι	I be able, to be capable of
ἐλεέω	I pity
εὑρίσκω	I find
λαλέω	I say, to tell
μένω	I stay, to remain
πιστεύω	I believe
πορεύομαι	I go
προσεύχομαι	I pray
σώζω	I save

Nouns

ἄρχων, -οντος, ὁ	ruler
ἐντολή, ῆς, ἡ	commandment

εὐαγγέλιον, -ου, τό	a gospel
λαός, -οῦ, ὁ	a people
ῥῆμα, -ατος, τό	a word
φαρισαῖος, -ου, ὁ	Pharisee
φυλακή, -ης, ἡ	guard, prison

You will find exercises for this lesson on page: 152

SECOND CLASS WORDS – PERFECT AND PLUPERFECT

Past tense

Greek has so many past tenses that a student could get pretty confused in no time. Actually the confusion comes from not keeping one important thing in mind: "tense", to the Greeks, meant more than *when* something happened. It also meant *what kind* of action it is. Thus when we translate a past tense Greek verb, we have to determine when it happened *and* what kind of action it was.

For example, imperfect tense verbs tell us about an action that was "in progress" – that is, something that was going on at a certain time, but we don't know whether it was finished (actually the emphasis is usually on something else in the sentence, rather than on the imperfect verb itself). Aorist, on the other hand, tells us about a completed action. Or you could say that the aorist is used for a nondescript action; it happened, and that's all.

But there are a couple of other possibilities for past tenses – and that's where the perfect and the pluperfect come in.

Perfect

When a Biblical writer uses the perfect, he's describing an action that is done – and it has present, real results. He's trying to show what happened *because of* the action. It could have happened in the past, or it might be a present action; but the results are real now (in respect to the writer, that is). For example, if we look at the sentence –

ὁ δέ διακρινόμενος ἐάν φάγη <u>κατακέκριται</u>

we can see that the underlined verb is in the perfect tense (I'll show you its characteristics in a minute). How do we translate this sentence? Like this:

But the one who judges <u>is condemned</u> if he eats.

Notice that the perfect verb talks about an action that has already happened – he is condemned as soon as he eats. But more importantly, it has present results – the condemnation, *because* he ate, is *still in force* over him. The perfect often looks like this.

Pluperfect

The pluperfect works just like the perfect does, except the action and the results of that action are all in the past. Neither one has anything to do with the present. The Greek pluperfect is rarely used in the New Testament; it's just one of those things that you'll have to remember when you meet up with it, and refer to your dictionary or grammar.

Conjugations

The dead give-away that you're looking at a perfect or pluperfect verb is the repeated letter on the front end of the word. For example:

verb: λύω   **stem**: λυ-   **perf**: λέλυκα   **pluperf**: λελύκειν

The repeated letter works every time. There's another clue there, which you may have noticed: both have the letter **κ** added onto the stem before the personal endings were tacked on. Only these two tenses have that characteristic in Greek. So it's really easy to spot perfect and pluperfect tenses.

Following is the verb λύω conjugated in the two tenses:

Perfect	**Pluperfect**
Singular	
λέλυκα (I have been loosed)	λελύκειν (I had been loosed)
λέλυκας	λελύκεις
λέλυκεν	λελύκει
Plural	
λελύκαμεν	λελύκειμεν
λελύκατε	λελύκειτε
λελύκασιν	λελύκεισαν

Vocabulary

Verbs

present	**perfect**	**pluperfect**	
βαπτίζω	βεβάπτικα	βεβάπτικειν	baptize
γίνομαι	γέγονα	ἐγέγονειν	beget
γινώσκω	ἔγνωκα	ἐγνώκειν	know
δίδωμι	δέδωκα	δέδωκειν	give
ζητέω	ζήτηκα	ἐζήτηκειν	seek
πληρόω	πεπλήρωκα	πετλήρωκειν	fill, fulfill
ποιέω	πέποικα	πετοίηκειν	do
τηρέω	τετήρηκα	τετήρηκειν	keep
φανερόω	πεφανέρωκα	πεφανέρωκειν	reveal

Nouns

γῆ, γῆς, ἡ	earth, land
δύναμις, -εως, ἡ	power
σωτηρία, -ας, ἡ	salvation
χείρ, χειρός, ἡ	hand

You will find exercises for this lesson on page: 159

INFINITIVES AND PARTICIPLES

A cross between two classes

Infinitives and participles are tricky kinds of words. Technically they're made from verbs; but the work that they do in a sentence could be noun or verbal work. In other words, they can be either first class or second class words, depending on how they're used in a sentence.

Infinitives usually act like nouns – they're often the direct object of a normal verb. And participles usually act like adjectives, describing a noun. Sometimes, though, the infinitive acts as a verb, and the participle will take the place of a noun. But the one thing to remember is this: they both are really verbs in new dress; we just have to check out their endings to find out what they're actually doing.

Infinitives – the theory

What's an infinitive? It's "unlimited action," "un-finite" action. That is, it's action that's not limited by tense. It's pure action, seen by itself and unhindered by trying to decide when it happened. For example, we can say "he ran." The indicative form "ran" tells us, by its tense, that the action of running happened awhile ago. But if we say, "to run," the verb "run" isn't described in such a way that we know when it might be happening – past, present, or future. It's pure action.

Note that in English an infinitive is expressed by two things: 1) the word "to", and 2) a verb. In Greek, also, we need two things to make an infinitive: 1) a verb stem, and 2) an ending for the stem (you expected that, right?).

Before we look at how to make an infinitive, I want to say one thing: Greek infinitives have present forms, aorist forms, and future forms. Now I know that I just said that infinitives don't have any tense; and I still say that they don't. But by making infinitives in these three forms we can use the infinitive to tell us a lot about the kind of action going on. Infinitives tell us nothing about tense; a present infinitive can be in the same sentence with an aorist main verb; or a future infinitive with a present main verb; and so on. The main verb determines the tense of the whole sentence, not the infinitive. But different infinitive forms can change the flavor of the main verb considerably. Basically it's like this:

Present infinitives	show	**Continuous** action
Aorist infinitives	show	**indefinite** action
Future infinitives	show	**unfulfilled** action

Let's take this sentence for an example:

I have not come to destroy.

Now let's make the three different forms for this infinitive:

- **I have not come to destroy (present infinitive)** –
  that is, destroying isn't what I'm doing in this world.

- **I have not come to destroy (aorist infinitive)** –
  that is, it wasn't my purpose to come here and destroy.

- **I have not come to destroy (future infinitive)** –
  that is, I'm not anticipating any destroying work to do.

You know, of course, that this comes from Matthew 5:17. Can you guess which form was used here? This is the Greek original:

οὐκ ἦλθον καταλῦσαι

It's the second form, the aorist infinitive – and it means that it wasn't Jesus' purpose to come and destroy the Law or the Prophets' message. That's quite a bit different from the meanings of the other two forms; we'd never have known the true meaning behind his words if it wasn't for "splitting hairs" and checking to see which infinitive form he actually used.

Infinitive endings

Following is the way we go about making the infinitives:

present infinitives	aorist infinitives	future infinitives
1 – find the verb stem	**1** – find the verb stem	**1** – find the verb stem
2 – add the letters -ϵιν	**2** – add the letter σ	**2** – add the letter σ
	3 – add the letters -αι	**3** – add the letters -ϵιν

λυ-	λυ-	λυ-
λύϵιν	λυσ-	λυσ-
	λῦσαι	λῦσϵιν

Notice that all three start with the stem. The present infinitive ends with the letters -ϵιν, and the future infinitive (as would be expected – see the lesson on future verbs) adds a σ onto the stem first. The aorist infinitive adds the usual aorist σ and the ending -αι.

One thing you probably won't mind: you can't decline or conjugate an infinitive, so these are the only endings you'll be learning!

Participles – verbal adjectives

Participles are often called ***verbal adjectives***, because they're really verbs that function as adjectives. English participles have the same characteristic. For example, these are some English participles: falling, crying, seeing. It's easy to use these to describe nouns: the falling star, the crying baby, the seeing eye.

But participles aren't always adjectives; they often act simply as nouns – subjects and objects. "Seeing is believing" is a famous example of participial nouns. "We like eating," or "Running is good for you," or "There's strength in believing" show how the participle is used as subject and object.

Since Greek participles are used as first class words, we have to be able to decline them like any noun or adjective. As an adjective, a participle has to agree with the noun that it's modifying in ***gender***, ***number***, and ***case***. So all participles have a three-column paradigm just like adjectives. Following is λύω changed into a participle and declined.

	masculine	feminine	neuter
Singular			
Nom.:	λύων	λύουσα	λῦον
Gen.:	λύοντος	λύουσης	λύοντος
Dat.:	λύοντι	λύουσῃ	λύοντι
Acc.:	λύοντα	λύουσαν	λῦον
Plural			
Nom.:	λύοντες	λύουσαι	λύοντα
Gen.:	λυόντων	λυουσῶν	λυόντων
Dat.:	λύουσιν	λυούσαις	λύουσιν
Acc.:	λύοντας	λυούσας	λύοντα

You should note a couple of things here: first, you can easily see that each gender uses a particular declension's endings. Masculine uses the third declension, feminine uses the first declension, and neuter uses the third declension.

Second, don't let participles mix you up. If you know your vocabulary, you'll know that what you're looking at is a **verb**, not a noun – no matter what kinds of endings are on it. Then all you have to do is ask it why it has noun endings on it – and you're well on your way to translating a participle.

Vocabulary

Nouns

αἷμα, -τος, ἡ	blood
δικαιοσύνη, -ης, ἡ	righteousness
θάνατος, -ου, ὁ	death
μήτηρ, -τρός, ἡ	mother
μυστήριον, -ου, τό	mystery
πόλις, -λεως, ἡ	city
πῦρ, πυρός, τό	fire
φωνή, -ῆς, ἡ	voice, sound
ψυχή, -ῆς, ἡ	life, soul

Verbs

ἀπιστέω	I fail to believe
δικαιόω	I declare or show righteousness
κράζω	I call out, shout
προλέγω	I warn, predict

Adjectives

ἐχθρός, ά, όν	enemy, hated

You will find exercises for this lesson on page: 165

Verb Chart showing full conjugations for verb λύω

		λύω				λύσω		ἔλυσα		λέλυκα		λέλυμαι	ἐλύθην	
		pres.a.	imp.a.	pres.m.p.	imp.m.p.	fut.a.	fut.m.p.	aor.a.	aor.m.	perf.a.	plup.a.	perf.m.p.	aor.p.	fut.p.
①	1	λύω	ἔλυον	λύομαι	ἐλυόμην	λύσω	λύσομαι	ἔλυσα	ἐλυσάμην	λέλυκα	(ἐ)λελύκειν	λέλυμαι	ἐλύθην	λυθήσομαι
	2	λύεις	ἔλυες	λύῃ	ἐλύου	λύσεις	λύσῃ	ἔλυσας	ἐλύσω	λέλυκας	(ἐ)λελύκεις	λέλυσαι	ἐλύθης	λυθήσῃ
	3	λύει	ἔλυεν	λύεται	ἐλύετο	λύσει	λύσεται	ἔλυσεν	ἐλύσατο	λέλυκεν	(ἐ)λελύκει	λέλυται	ἐλύθη	λυθήσεται
	1	λύομεν	ἐλύομεν	λυόμεθα	ἐλυόμεθα	λύσομεν	λυσόμεθα	ἐλύσαμεν	ἐλυσάμεθα	λελύκαμεν	(ἐ)λελύκειμεν	λελύμεθα	ἐλύθημεν	λυθησόμεθα
	2	λύετε	ἐλύετε	λύεσθε	ἐλύεσθε	λύσετε	λύσεσθε	ἐλύσατε	ἐλύσασθε	λελύκατε	(ἐ)λελύκειτε	λέλυσθε	ἐλύθητε	λυθήσεσθε
	3	λύουσιν	ἔλυον	λύονται	ἐλύοντο	λύσουσιν	λύσονται	ἔλυσαν	ἐλύσαντο	λελύκασιν λέλυκαν	(ἐ)λελύκεισαν	λέλυνται	ἐλύθησαν	λυθήσονται
②	1	λύω		λύωμαι				λύσω	λύσωμαι				λυθῶ	
	2	λύῃς		λύῃ				λύσῃς	λύσῃ				λυθῇς	
	3	λύῃ		λύηται				λύσῃ	λύσηται				λυθῇ	
	1	λύωμεν		λυώμεθα				λύσωμεν	λυσώμεθα				λυθῶμεν	
	2	λύητε		λύησθε				λύσητε	λύσησθε				λυθῆτε	
	3	λύωσιν		λύωνται				λύσωσιν	λύσωνται				λυθῶσιν	
③	2	λῦε		λύου				λῦσον	λῦσαι				λύθητι	
	3	λυέτω		λυέσθω				λυσάτω	λυσάσθω				λυθήτω	
	2	λύετε		λύεσθε				λύσατε	λύσασθε				λύθητε	
	3	λυέτωσαν		λυέσθωσαν				λυσάτωσαν	λυσάσθωσαν				λυθήτωσαν	
④		λύειν		λύεσθαι				λῦσαι	λύσασθαι	λελυκέναι		λελύσθαι	λυθῆναι	
⑤		λύων		λυόμενος				λύσας	λυσάμενος	λελυκώς		λελυμένος	λυθείς	
		λύουσα		λυομένη				λύσασα	λυσαμένη	λελυκυῖα		λελυμένη	λυθεῖσα	
		λῦον		λυόμενον				λῦσαν	λυσάμενον	λελυκός		λελυμένον	λυθέν	

Taken from *New Testament Greek for Beginners*, J. Gresham Machen, The MacMillan Company, 1941; p. 238.

SECOND CLASS WORDS – VERB CHART, ODDBALL VERBS

Greek Verb Chart

If one were to collect all the different verb forms together into a handy chart, it would really help us see what possible endings a verb could have. So, on the facing page you see just such a chart using the Greek verb λύω as a model of the "perfect" verb. Each column of forms has a basic verb that it builds all its additional forms from – called a *principle part*. For example, all the verbs in the first group of four columns come from the verb λύω; all the second group (two columns) build up from the verb λύσω; and so on. If you know the principle parts well (after all, there are only 6 of them! – they're printed across the top of the page) and you're pretty good at guessing the person that the ending is for, then you can really narrow down a strange verb in a text somewhere and get a good idea about its grammar.

Also note that the chart shows all five *moods* of the verb: the indicative ①, the subjunctive ②, the imperative ③, the infinitive ④, and the participle ⑤.

Oddball verbs

Every language has them. There are just some verbs that don't follow the rules – and, unfortunately, these verbs are used a lot in ordinary speech. Greek has them too. There are three kinds of oddball Greek verbs that we'll look at here.

Mi-verbs. Some verbs are called Mi-verbs because the first person, singular, active, present form of the verb ends in the letters **μι** instead of the regular **ω**. Why? Don't ask! It's just that some words came down through history in that form.

The conjugation of Mi-verbs is a little different from normal, as you might expect. Following is a chart of the popular Mi-verb, δίδωμι – "I give".

	Pres.act.	imperf.act.	pres.m.p.	imperf.m.p.
Singular				
1	δίδωμι	ἐδίδουν	δίδομαι	ἐδιδόμειν
2	δίδως	ἐδίδου	δίδοσαι	ἐδίδοσο
3	δίδωσιν	ἐδίδου	δίδοται	ἐδίδοτο
Plural				
1	δίδομεν	ἐδιδόμεν	διδόμεθα	ἐδιδόμεθα
2	δίδοτε	ἐδίδοτε	δίδοσθε	ἐδίδοσθε
3	διδόασιν	ἐδίδοσαν	δίδονται	ἐδίδοντο

Contract verbs. Some verbs have a stem that ends in a vowel. Remember, most of the verbs that we've been looking at so far have stems that end in a consonant, like βαπτίζω – its stem is βαπτίζ- (for some reason, λύω doesn't give any problem). But take a word like τιμάω, with a stem of τιμά-. Let's add the second person ending on this stem: τιμάεις. See those three vowels all together? Now let's shorten, or **contract**, the three vowels into one vowel: τιμάς. This eliminates a lot of unnecessary letters. It reminds us of the vowel contractions that we had to learn for the nouns in earlier lessons.

Here's a chart that shows what the contract verb endings will be when you add personal endings:

2) ... and your personal ending has:

		ε	ει	η	η	ο	ου	ω
1) If the stem	α	α	α	α	α	ω	ω	ω
ends in –	ε	ει	ει	η	η	ου	ου	ω
	ο	ου	οι	ω	οι	ου	ου	ω

3) ... then contract the vowels into these!

(**Note**: Really, you won't be contracting the verbs when you translate the New Testament – you'll only need to know the popular contract verbs and *why* they have their peculiar endings when you run across them in the text.)

Deponent verbs. Some verbs are completely messed up. They seem to break all the rules and yet they're used very often. We'll just have to learn the most popular ones and be warned that they aren't going to look like what they're supposed to look like.

"Deponent" means that the verb has a middle or passive ending (see the verb chart) and yet it's translated with an active meaning. For example, the word γίνομαι, which means "to become." By rights, γίνομαι should mean "I become myself," meaning that I make myself (that's how middle verbs are translated). But it doesn't mean that; it's to be translated simply "I become." In the same crazy vein, this verb's aorist form is also deponent: ἐγενόμην means "I have become," quite an un-middle translation.

Some verbs are deponent in only one tense, like ἔρχομαι. The present form, as you can see, is middle but translated as present; its aorist form, however, is ἦλθον, "I came." That's a normal aorist ending. So you just have to get used to these popular deponent verbs and expect anything. Just have your dictionary handy.

Imperative mood

We haven't said anything yet about the imperative mood, but there's not much to say. *Imperative* means "command" – the speaker tells someone to do something.

In Greek, there are only two tenses for the imperative – the present and the aorist; but it's almost impossible to see any difference between their translation.

There are also only two persons: second and third. But the imperative does come in all three voices: active, middle, and passive.

You can check out the forms for the imperative on the verb chart.

Vocabulary

MI-verbs

δίδωμι	I give
ἵστημι	I stand
τίθημι	I put

Contract verbs

ἀγαπάω	I love
πληρόω	I fulfill
ποιέω	I do, I make
τιμάω	I honor

Deponent verbs

present	future	aorist	
γίνομαι	γενήσομαι	ἐγενόμην	become
ἔρχομαι	ἐλεύσομαι	ἦλθον	come
γινώσκω	γνώσομαι	ἔγνων	know
λαμβάνω	λήμψομαι	ἔλαβον	take, receive

Nouns

ἐξουσία, -ας, ἡ	authority

You will find exercises for this lesson on page: 172

FINAL NOTES

Grammars

This winds up our Greek course. Now you have the basics to start working in your Greek Bible on your own. I hope you realize that I only gave you the rock-bottom basics of *koine* Greek. The reason I did that was because you don't need a high-powered grammar when all you'll be doing is translating a short passage once in a while from the Bible.

But you will inevitably run into something you're not familiar with. For example, in the first verse of the Gospel of John, we immediately run into a technical problem that a student wouldn't even know about unless he looked it up in a complete grammar:

καὶ θεός ἦν ὁ λόγος

Literally, this means "and God was the Word." But there's a rule in Greek that if two nouns are in the sentence, and the verb is the word "to be", and only one of the nouns has an article attached – *that* noun is the subject, no matter what place it has in the sentence. So in this sentence, λόγος is the noun; θεός is placed first only for emphasis. What it's saying is that the Word is *God and nothing less than God*. (This becomes important, for example, when you talk to a group like the Jehovah's Witnesses. Their translation deliberately ignores this grammar rule and translates this sentence incorrectly; they don't want any passage to teach that Jesus is God!)

So I recommend that you pick up a good Greek grammar and use it for reference; you'll need it.

Here are some good grammars that you might want to look at:

Basics of Biblical Greek Grammar, William D. Mounce; Zondervan, 2009.

A Manual Grammar of the Greek New Testament, H.E.Dana and J.R. Mantey; MacMillan, 1955. (Highly recommended as a handy little reference for Greek grammar – *very* complete.)

New Testament Greek For Beginners, J. Gresham Machen; MacMillan, 1941.

With one of these grammar books, a lexicon, these notes, and your Greek Bible, you should be able to translate most anything in the New Testament.

Translations

Next, we should look at the problem of translating. Every Christian wants to have as exact a translation of the original as possible. The only thing about that is, that's not possible. I mean, there's usually more than one way to translate a word or phrase – and any of them may be valid translations. For example, let's take a look at John 1:5 –

$$καί \ ἡ \ σκοτία \ αὐτό \ οὐ \ κατέλαβεν$$

The word κατέλαβεν is in the aorist tense, from καταλαμβάνω, which means to seize, grasp, comprehend, make one's own, overcome, overtake, catch, or understand. Now which meaning should we use here? Either the darkness did violence to the light, or it failed to overtake it, or it couldn't understand it.

This is why there are so many translations on the market today – for the simple reason that there are so many ways to translate the same text. And usually the translations each render the text in a valid way. Now, of course, you don't have to rely on their interpretation; but don't be foolish and ignore all their hard work! What they see there may just help you find a meaning that you need.

Remember also about the idioms. Idioms are peculiar ways that people have of saying things; an idiom doesn't really mean what it says literally. We already looked at one idiom (John 2:4)

$$τί \ ἐμοί \ καί \ σοί, \ γύναι;$$

Literally, he's *saying* "What to me and to you, woman?" What he *means* is, "What does their being out of wine have to do with us, Mother?" We would use different words to arrive at that meaning, however. For example, here is how several translations try to handle this idiomatic phrase:

Dear woman, why do you involve me? (NIV)

Woman, what have I to do with thee? (KJV)

You must not tell me what to do. (TEV)

The New Testament is full of idioms, and you should be on the lookout for these strange expressions.

The manuscript problem

As you know, there are thousands of manuscripts around of the Greek New Testament. Your Greek Bible tells you something of what the most important manuscripts say about any particular passage. It's up to you to pass judgment on the choices; but at least the editor gives you all the choices at the bottom of the page so that you can make up your own mind as to how it should read.

Here's what's on the bottom of a page from the Greek text prepared by Aland, et.al. (United Bible Societies, 2nd Ed. 1968)

---

[7] **33** {D} *αὐτων ἡμιν* C^3 E P 049 056 0142 33 81 88 104 181 326 330 436 451 614 630 945 1241 1505 1739 1877 2127 2412 2492 2495 Byz Lect^m l^{1443} it^e (syr^{p,h}) arm geo Chrysostom Cosmas Greek$^{acc.to Bede}$ Theophylact // *ἡμιν* 142 // *ἡμων* p^{74} a A B C* D it^{ar,c,d,t} vg eth Hilary Ambrose Cosmas // *ὑμων* Y it^p // *αὐτων* 629 it^{gig} cop$^{sa,bo.mss}$ Ambrose // omit cop$^{bo.mss}$

It's a footnote for Acts 13:33. The problem is whether to translate it "... he has fulfilled for us, **their** children" or "... he has fulfilled for us, **the** children". The first set of manuscripts (up to the first // marks) *do* have the word "their", and the rest of them *don't* — they just have various forms of the word "for us." The last one omits the entire phrase and makes it read "for the children". (The numbers represent individual manuscripts — they can keep track of them better that way.) Which manuscripts are right? The "D" at the beginning is the scale of difficulty in trying to decide what the correct reading is. Since there are *very* dependable manuscripts that disagree here, the scholars could only make an educated guess about which one to use. If they would have put "A", this means that all the good manuscripts agree on a certain reading and the less dependable manuscripts disagree. "B" and "C" would mean there is more doubt about it.

This should give you an idea about how difficult it is for translators and Greek scholars to discover how the original autographs really read. But it also shows you the nature of the problem: none of the variations are about points of doctrine, or things that should divide Christians. Fortunately, the Bible is the best preserved document in all of history; in comparison, other ancient books, like Homer's stories, vary so widely from copy to copy that you would think that they were almost two different stories!

VOCABULARY

ἀγαπάω	I love	γινώσκω	I know
ἀγάπη, -ης, ἡ	love	γραμματεύς, -έως, ὁ	scribe
ἄγγελος, -ου, ὁ	angel	γράφω	I write
ἅγιος, α, ον	holy		
ἀγρός, -οῦ, ὁ	a field	γυνή, γυναικός, ἡ	woman
ἄγω	I lead		
ἀδελφή, -ῆς, ἡ	sister	δαίμων, -ονος, ὁ	demon
ἀδελφός, -οῦ, ὁ	brother	δέ	but, and
αἷμα, -τος, τό	blood	διδάσκαλος, -ου, ὁ	teacher
αἴρω	I take	διδάσκω	I teach
αἰτέω	I ask	δίδωμι	I give
ἀκολουθέω	I follow	δίκαιος, α, ον	righteous
ἀκούω	I hear	δικαιοσύνη, ης, ἡ	righteousness
ἀληθῶς	truly	δικαιόω	I declare righteous
ἀλήθεια, -ας, ἡ,	truth	διώκω	I persecute
ἀλλά	but	δόξα, -ης, ἡ	glory
ἄλλος, η, ο	other	δύναμαι	I am able
ἁμαρτία, -ας, ἡ	sin	δύναμις, -εως, ἡ	power
ἁμαρτωλός, ή, όν	sinful	δῶρον, -ου, τό	a gift
ἀμήν	truly		
ἀνήρ, ἀνδρός, ὁ	man	ἐγείρω	I raise up
ἄνθρωπος, -ου, ὁ	man	ἐγώ	I
ἀνοίγω	I open	εἰρήνη, -ης, ἡ	peace
ἄνωθεν	from above	εἰσίν	they are
ἀπιστέω	I don't believe	ἐκεῖ	there
ἀποθνήσκω	I die	ἐκκλησία, -ας, ἡ	church
ἀποκρίνομαι	I answer	ἐλεέω	I pity
ἀποκτείνω	I kill	ἐλπίς, -ίδος, ἡ	hope
ἀποστέλλω	I send	ἐλπίζω	I hope
ἆρα	then	ἐντολή, ῆς, ἡ	commandment
ἄρτι	now	ἐξουσία, -ας, ἡ	authority
ἄρτος, -ου, ὁ	bread, a loaf	ἔργον, -ου, τό	work
ἀρχή, -ῆς, ἡ	beginning	ἔρχομαι	I come
ἄρχων, -οντος, ὁ	ruler	ἐσθίω	I eat
		ἐστίν	he, she, or it is
βαπτίζω	I baptize	ἔσχατος, η, ον	last
βασιλεία, -ας, ἡ	kingdom	εὐαγγέλιον, -ου, τό	a gospel
βιβλίον, -ου, τό	book	εὑρίσκω	I find
βλέπω	I see	εὐχαριστέω	I give thanks
		ἐχθρός, ά, όν	enemy, hated
γάρ	for	ἔχω	I have
γῆ, γῆς, ἡ	earth, land		
γίνομαι	I become, beget	ζαω	I live

ζητέω	I seek	μένω	I remain
ζωή, -ῆς, ἡ	life	μή	no, not
		μήτηρ, -τρός, ἡ	mother
ἤ	or	μικρός, α, ον	small
ἡμέρα, -ας, ἡ	day	μυστήριον, -ου, τό	mystery
θάλασσα, -ης, ἡ	sea, lake	νεκρός, ά, όν	dead
θάνατος, -ου, ὁ	death	νόμος, -ου, ὁ	law
θέλω	I wish	νῦν	now
Θεός, -ου, ὁ	God	νύξ, νυκτός, ἡ	night
Ἰάκωβος, -ου, ὁ	James	οἰκία, -ας, ἡ	house
ἴδιος, α, ον	one's own	ὄνομα, ὀνόματος, τό	name
ἱερόν, -οῦ, τό	a temple	ὄντως	really
Ἰησοῦς, -ου, ὁ	Jesus	ὅπου	where
ἱκανός, ή, όν	sufficient	οὐ, οὐκ	no, not
ἱμάτιον, -οῦ, τό	garment	οὐδέποτε	never
Ἰουδαῖος, α, ον	Jewish	οὖν	so, therefore
ἵστημι	I stand	οὔπω	not yet
ἰχθύς, -θύος, ὁ	fish	οὐρανός, -οῦ, ὁ	heaven
		οὔτε	nor
καθώς	as	ὀφείλω	I owe
καί	and	ὀφθαλμός, -οῦ, ὁ	eye
κακός, ή, όν	bad	ὄχλος, -ου, ὁ	crowd
καλός, ά, όν	good		
καλύπτω	I hide	πάλιν	again
καρδία, -ας, ἡ	heart	πάντοτε	always
κελεύω	I command	πάσχω	I suffer
κηρύσσω	I preach	πατήρ, πατρός, ὁ	father
κόσμος, -ου, ὁ	world	πείθω	I persuade
κράζω	I call out	πειράζω	I tempt
κρίνω	I judge	πέμπω	I send
κύριος, -ου, ὁ	Lord	περιπατέω	I walk
κώμη, -ης, ἡ	village	Πέτρος, -ου, ὁ	Peter
		πιστεύω	I believe
λαλέω	I say, tell	πιστός, η, ον	faithful
λαμβάνω	I take, receive	πληρόω	I fill, fulfill
λαός, -οῦ, ὁ	a people	πλοῖον, -ου, τό	a boat
λέγω	I tell	πνεῦμα, -ματος, τό	spirit
λίθος, -ου, ὁ	a stone	ποιέω	I do, I make
λόγος, -ου, ὁ	word	πόλις, -λεως, ἡ	city
λύω	I loose	πονηρός, ά, όν	sinful, wicked
		πορεύομαι	to go
μαθητής, -οῦ, ὁ	disciple	πρεσβύτερος, α, ον	older, elder
μακάριος, α, ον	blessed, happy	προλέγω	I predict
μαρτυρία, -ας, ἡ	witness	προσεύχομαι	I pray
μετανοέω	I repent	προφήτης, -ου, ὁ	prophet

πρῶτον	first		
πῦρ, πυρός, τό	fire	ὕδωρ, ὕδατος, τό	water
		υἱός, -οῦ, ὁ	son
ῥῆμα, -ατος, τό	a word	ὑποστρέφω	I return
σάρξ, σαρκός, ἡ	flesh	φανερόω	I reveal
σκοτία, -ας, ἡ	darkness	φαρισαῖος, -ου, ὁ	Pharisee
στρατιώτης, -ου, ὁ	soldier	φυλακή, -ης, ἡ	guard, prison
συναγωγή, -ῆς, ἡ	synagogue	φωνή, -ής, ἡ	voice, sound
σῶμα, -ματος, ἡ	body	φῶς, φωτός, τό	light
σώτηρ, -ῆρος, ὁ	savior		
σωτηρία, -ας, ἡ	salvation	χαίρω	I rejoice
		χαρά, ἡ	joy
σώζω	I save	χάρις, χάριστος, ἡ	grace
		χείρ, χειρός, ἡ	hand
τέ	and	Χριστός, -οῦ, ὁ	Christ
τέκνον, -ου, τό	child		
τηρέω	I keep	ψυχή, -ῆς, ἡ	life, soul
τίθημι	I put		
τιμάω	I honor	ὥρα, -ας, ἡ	hour
τιμή, -ῆς, ἡ	honor	ὡς	that
τότε	then		

EXERCISES

EXERCISES FOR
FIRST CLASS WORDS – NOUNS

For each of the following words, write the stem and the ending. Do it as in the example:

Example: λόγου   **stem:** λόγ-   **ending:** -ου

	stem	ending
Χριστῷ		
νόμοι		
Ἰάκωβον		
Χριστῶν		
κόσμους		
Ἰησῷ		
Πέτρον		
λόγῳ		
ἄνθρωπος		
Ἰακώβου		
Ἰακώβῳ		
Πέτρος		
λόγων		
κόσμον		
Πέτρου		
Θεοῖς		
κόσμων		
Θεός		
λόγους		
Χριστός		
Θεοῦ		
κόσμῳ		
Ἰάκωβος		
ἀνθρώποις		
Θεῷ		

Tell the case and number for each of the following words:

	case	number
Χριστός		
Ἰησῷ		
Ἰάκωβῳ		
Θεοῦ		
Χριστῷ		
κόσμῳ		
Πέτρον		
Ἰάκωβον		
κόσμοις		
λόγῳ		
Χριστόν		
Θεούς		
Πέτρος		
λόγοι		
Χριστῷ		
λόγοις		
ἀνθρώποις		
Θεῷ		
κόσμον		
νόμοι		
Πέτρου		
Πέτρῳ		
κόσμου		
κόσμων		
νόμον		
Θεός		
νόμοι		

Finish each of the following sentences with the appropriate Greek word (don't worry about the articles for now) Adjectives must have the same ending as the noun they describe: for example –

The world is bad – κόσμ<u>ος</u> ἐστίν πονηρ<u>ός</u>

Peter loves _____ (God).

Jesus is _____ (good).

The men love the _____ (word).

The world is _____ (dead).

Peter and James love _____ (Jesus).

Jesus' _____ (word) is good.

God loves _____ (men).

The law _____ (of God) is holy.

Christ Jesus is _____ (a good God).

Christ's _____ (law) is holy.

Peter loves _____ (Jesus and James).

The _____ (words)

  _____ (of men) are bad.

The bad _____ (men) are dead.

Peter and James are _____ (good men).

Translate the following sentences into English:

᾿Ιάκωβος και Πέτρος εἰσίν ἄνθρωποι καλοί.

Πέτρος και ᾿Ιάκωβος ἀγαπούσιν Θεόν.

Κόσμος καλός ἐστίν κόσμος ἅγιος.

Κόσμος πονηρός ἐστίν νεκρός.

Πονηροί λόγοι ἀνθρῶπων οὐκ (not) εἰσίν ἅγιοι.

Θεός ἀγαπά λόγους καλούς.

᾿Ιησοῦς ἐστίν Χριστός.

Λόγοι ἄνθρωποι εἰσίν ἅγιοι.

Θεός ἀγαπά νόμον καλόν.

᾿Ιάκωβος οὐκ ἀγαπά κόσμον.

Translate the following sentences into Greek:

God loves Peter and James.

Jesus is a holy God.

Dead men are not (οὐκ) good.

The word of God is good and holy.

The world of God is holy.

God loves the world.

Bad men don't (οὐκ) love Christ.

Good men love God and Christ.

James is a holy man.

Holy men love the law.

Here are the first five verses of the Gospel of John. You don't have to translate them, but at least study them and find all the *second declension* nouns that you can. Remember, you find them by looking for the distinctive endings of the second declension. When you find them, tell what case and number they are, and then look them up in the dictionary and find their meaning. Be careful – there are a few other words with second declension endings on them, but they aren't nouns! (*Hint*: there are *seven* words!)

’Εν ἀρχῇ ἦν ὁ λόγος, καὶ ὁ λόγος ἦν πρὸς τὸν θεόν, καὶ θεὸς ἦν
ὁ λόγος. ²οὗτος ἦν ἐν ἀρχῇ πρὸς τὸν θεόν.

³πάντα δί αὐτοῦ ἐγένετο, καὶ χωρὶς αὐτοῦ ἐγένετο
οὐδὲ ἕν ὃ γέγονεν. ⁴ἐν αὐτῷ ζωὴ ἦν, καὶ ἡ ζωὴ ἦν τὸ φῶς τῶν
ἀνθρώπων, ⁵καὶ τὸ φῶς ἐν τῇ σκοτίᾳ φαίνει, καὶ ἡ
σκοτία αὐτὸ οὐ κατέλαβεν.

EXERCISES FOR
FIRST CLASS WORDS – NOUNS (PART 2)

For each of the following words, write the stem, the ending, and the case. Do it as in the example:

Example:	ἀγάπης	stem: ἀγάπ-	ending: -ης	case: Gen.
	τέκνοις			
	μαθητήν			
	ἀρχήν			
	ἀδελφῇ			
	ζωῶν			
	ὥραις			
	ἀλήθειαν			
	ἀρχῇ			
	δόξᾳ			
	ἐκκλησίας			
	προφήταις			
	τέκνῳ			
	ἐκκλησίᾳ			
	τιμήν			
	ζωαί			
	δόξας			
	μαθηταί			
	προφήτου			
	ἀδελφῶν			
	σκοτία			
	ἀληθείας			
	τιμῶν			
	ὥρας			
	σκοτίαι			

Tell the case, number, and declension for each of the following words:

	case	number	declension
τέκνον			
δόξα			
ἀρχήν			
μαθητής			
τιμάς			
ἀδελφήν			
σκοτίαις			
ἀλήθειαις			
ἀρχῶν			
ὥρᾳ			
δόξαν			
ἐκκλησίαις			
τέκνων			
ζωῆς			
μαθηταίς			
προφήτην			
σκοτίας			
ἐκκλησίαν			
ἀλήθειαι			
τιμῆς			
προφήτης			
ζωῇ			
ἀδελφῆς			
ὥραν			

Finish each of the following sentences with the appropriate Greek word (don't worry about the articles for now) Adjectives must have the same ending as the noun they describe: for example –

The truth is good – ζωή ἐστίν καλή

God loves the _____ (church's) life.

The prophet sees _____ (darkness).

The _____ (child of God) loves life.

Honor is good for the _____ (disciples)

_____ (of Christ).

Truth will be the _____ (beginning) of honor.

The world doesn't love the _____ (disciples).

The witness sees the _____ (hour)

_____ (of the church).

_____ (Prophets) and

_____ (witnesses) love Christ.

God loves _____ (holy sisters).

The disciple of _____ (Peter) will be the

_____ (disciple of Christ).

_____ (Love) sees

_____ (the truth of God).

Translate the following sentences into English (don't worry for now about the endings of the adjectives):

Εἰμί μαρτυρία Χριστοῦ καί ἀλήθειας.

Τέκνον πονηρόν οὐκ ἀγαπά τιμήν.

Προφήται βλέπουσιν Θεόν και Χριστόν.

Μαθηταί βλέπουσιν δόξαν Θεοῦ.

Ἐκκλησία ἤν δόξα Ἰησοῦ.

Ζωή ἐστίν καλή, δέ σκοτία ἐστίν πονηρά.

Ἀδελφαί καλαί βλέπουσιν τέκνα δέ οὐκ ἀγαπούσιν σκοτίαν.

Τιμή Θεοῦ ἔσται ζωή καί ἀγάπη.

Κόσμος ἀγαπά σκοτίαν, δέ μαθηταί ἄγιοι βλέπουσιν ἀλήθειαν.

Ἀγάπη ἐστίν καλή, καί τιμή ἐστίν κάλη, δέ σκοτία οὐκ ἀγαπά Χριστόν.

Translate the following sentences into Greek:

Bad men love darkness.

God's honor is the beginning of glory.

The sisters and the witness love truth.

The disciple doesn't see the witnesses.

The life of Christ is the life of the Church.

The holy men love God and see life.

I will be holy and you will be holy.

The witnesses see Christ and the disciples.

The hour of the beginning was life.

The glory of the church is truth, but bad men do not love truth.

Here again are the first five verses of the Gospel of John. You don't have to translate them, but at least study them and find all the *first declension* nouns that you can. Remember, you find them by looking for the distinctive endings of the first declension. When you find them, tell what case and number they are, and then look them up in the dictionary and find their meaning. Be careful – there are a few other words with first declension endings on them, but they aren't nouns! (*Hint*: there are *six* words!)

Ἐν ἀρχῇ ἦν ὁ λόγος, καὶ ὁ λόγος ἦν πρὸς τὸν θεόν, καὶ θεὸς ἦν ὁ λόγος. ²οὗτος ἦν ἐν ἀρχῇ πρὸς τὸν θεόν.

³πάντα δί αὐτοῦ ἐγένετο, καὶ χωρὶς αὐτοῦ ἐγένετο οὐδὲ ἕν ὃ γέγονεν. ⁴ἐν αὐτῷ ζωὴ ἦν, καὶ ἡ ζωὴ ἦν τὸ φῶς τῶν ἀνθρώπων, ⁵καὶ τὸ φῶς ἐν τῇ σκοτίᾳ φαίνει, καὶ ἡ σκοτία αὐτὸ οὐ κατέλαβεν.

EXERCISES FOR
SECOND CLASS WORDS – VERBS

For each of the following words, write the stem and the ending. Do it as in the example:

Example: βαπτίζει   **stem**: βαπτίζ-   **ending**: -ει

ἄξουσιν

διώκει

γράφει

γράψω

βλεψουσιν

πείσουσιν

πέμψουσιν

ἄγει

βαπτίσει

διώκεις

γράφεις

βλεπει

βλεπετε

πείθετε

πέμπετε

ἄγομεν

βαπτίσομεν

διώκουσιν

γράφουσιν

βλεπομεν

πείθομεν

πέμπομεν

Tell the person, number, and tense for each of the following words:

	person	number	tense
ἄγουσιν			
βαπτίσουσιν			
διώξει			
γράψει			
βλεπουσιν			
πείθουσιν			
πέμπουσιν			
ἄξει			
βαπτίζεις			
διώξεις			
γράψεις			
βλεψει			
πείσει			
γράψετε			
βλεψεις			
πείσεις			
πέμψεις			
γράψομεν			
βλεψετε			
πείσετε			
πέμψετε			
ἄξομεν			
βαπτίζουσιν			
διώξουσιν			
γράψουσιν			
βλεψομεν			
πεισομεν			
πεμψομεν			

Finish each of the following sentences with the appropriate Greek verb.

The evil men _____ (persecute) the Church.

Peter and James _____ (will baptize) the sisters.

Jesus _____ (will persuade) the disciples.

God _____ (will lead) his people.

I know that _____ (you will send) the boys.

Paul _____ (will not baptize) any more people.

The disciples _____ (write) the Gospels.

Peter _____ (will loose) the boat.

God _____ (persuades) his people.

_____ (You [pl] are baptizing) the disciples.

_____ (We will write) our stories.

The disciples _____ (are baptizing) the people.

God _____ (looses) men from death.

_____ (You are leading) the Church.

God says, "_____ (I send) you to the Gentiles."

Translate the following sentences into English:

Ἄνθρωποι καλοί πέμπουσιν Πέτρον.

Θεός πείσει Πέτρον καί ἄξει Ἰάκωβον.

Ἰησούς ἀγαπά μαθητάς καί βαπτίσει ἐκκλησίαν.

Βασιλεία Θεοῦ ἐστίν καλή, καί μαθηταί πείθουσιν ἀνθρώπους.

Ὄχλος ἐστίν πονηρός, οὐν πείσω ὄχλον.

Πέτρος γραψει ἀληθείαν, τότε Ἰάκωβος βαπτίσει ἀδελφάς.

Ἰάκωβος ουκ γραφει νόμον, Ἰάκωβος γραφει ἀγάπην Θεοῦ.

Κόσμος πονηρός οὐκ ἀγαπά Θεόν.

Ἐκκλησία βλέπει δόξαν Θεοῦ και Χρίστου.

Translate the following sentences into Greek:

The prophets persuade men, and men see the truth of Christ.

The honor of the Son is the life of the Church.

Wicked men do not love the holy sisters.

The man's son will see the glory of Jesus.

Work is good, therefore you will write the truth.

God loves Christ as Jesus loves the Church.

I love the Church, therefore I will love holy men.

You (pl) will see the crowd as I see the darkness.

The disciples will write the truth, and they will see God.

Crowds of men are the beginning of an evil hour.

Here again are the first five verses of the Gospel of John, but this time I want you to find the *present verb*. Remember, you find it by looking for the distinctive endings of the present conjugation. When you find it, tell what person and number it is, and then look it up in the dictionary and find the meaning.

Ἐν ἀρχῇ ἦν ὁ λόγος, καὶ ὁ λόγος ἦν πρὸς τὸν θεόν, καὶ θεὸς ἦν ὁ λόγος. ²οὗτος ἦν ἐν ἀρχῇ πρὸς τὸν θεόν.

³πάντα δί αὐτοῦ ἐγένετο, καὶ χωρὶς αὐτοῦ ἐγένετο οὐδὲ ἕν ὃ γέγονεν. ⁴ἐν αὐτῷ ζωὴ ἦν, καὶ ἡ ζωὴ ἦν τὸ φῶς τῶν ἀνθρώπων, ⁵καὶ τὸ φῶς ἐν τῇ σκοτίᾳ φαίνει, καὶ ἡ σκοτία αὐτὸ οὐ κατέλαβεν.

EXERCISES FOR
OTHER FIRST CLASS WORDS – PRONOUNS, ADJECTIVES, ARTICLES

Tell the case, number, and gender of the following words:

	case	number	gender
αὐτοί			
καλούς			
καλῷ			
τάς			
τῆς			
αὐτός			
αὐτῶν			
καλαί			
καλόν			
τά			
τῇ			
αὐτοῖς			
αὐτοῦ			
καλαῖς			
καλή			
τήν			
αὐτούς			
αὐτῷ			
καλάς			
καλῆς			
τό			
αὐταί			
αὐτόν			
καλά			
καλῇ			

	case	number	gender
οἱ			
αὐταῖς			
αὐτή			
καλήν			
ὁ			
τῶν			
αὐτάς			
αὐτῆς			
καλόν			
τοῖς			
τοῦ			
αὐτά			
αὐτῇ			
καλοί			
τούς			
τῷ			
αἱ			
αὐτήν			
καλός			
καλῶν			
τόν			
αὐτό			
ἡ			
καλοῖς			
καλοῦ			
ταῖς			

Translate the following phrases into English:

ἅγιος ὁ ἄνθρωπος

ὁ Θεός ὁ ἅγιος

ὁ ὄχλος πονηρός

πρεσβύτερα ἡ ἀδελφή

ὁ μακάριος ὁ μαθητής

ὁ ἀδελφοί ἴδιοι

ἡ καρδία καλή

ἅγιος ὁ οὐρανός

ἄγγελοι οἱ δίκαιοι

ὁ κόσμος νεκρός

προφήτης ὁ μικρός

ὁ νεκρός ὁ κόσμος πονηρός

αἱ ἀδελφαί ἅγιαι αἱ μακάριαι

Θεός Θεός ὁ καλός

πονηροί οἱ ἄνθρωποι οἱ νεκροί

Πέτρος ὁ δίκαιος καί ὁ μακάριος

ὁ Ἰάκωβος μακάριος

ἡ καλή ἡ βασιλεία μακάρια

πονηροί οἱ υἱοί ἀνθρῶπων

σκοτία ἡ πονηρά

Translate the following sentences into English:

Ὁ ὄχλος ἀποκτενεῖ ἀνθρώπους πονηρούς.

Μαθηταί δίκαιοι ἀκολυθέουσιν Ἰησούς, δε ἄνθρωποι πονηροί ἀκολυθέουσιν ἄγγελον πονηρόν.

οἵ καλοί νόμοι λύσουσιν τήν σκοτίαν.

ὁ μακάριος ἄγγελος πέμψει τόν μακάριον προφέτην.

ἡ δίκαια ἐκκλησία ἀγαπώ τόν μικρόν ἔργον.

ἄγιος Ἰάκωβος πέμψει ἠν καλήν μαρτυρίαν.

ὁ δίκαιος ὄχλος βλέψει τόν πονηρόν τέκνον.

ἡ ἄγια βασιλεία γράψει τόν δίκαιον λόγον.

ὁ καλός ἄγγελος πείσει τόν μακάριον ὄχλον.

Δίκαιος Ἰησούς ἄξει τήν ἐκκλησίαν.

Translate the following sentences into Greek:

Bad days follow good beginnings.

The bad men persecute the good crowds.

Good men see heaven.

Righteous Jesus loves the blessed heart.

The older disciple will send good truth.

The good prophets persuade the righteous brothers.

The blessed prophets baptize the small sisters.

The holy prophets will be good disciples.

Righteous Christ will send older James.

The righteous truth will persuade one's own children.

Now you should be able to pick up a lot more words from the first five verses of the Gospel of John. Find the articles, adjectives, and pronouns. They will be both *first* and *second declension* words. Remember, you find them by looking for the distinctive endings of whatever declension it is part of. When you find them, tell what case and number they are, and then look them up in the dictionary and find their meaning.

Notice too that I spaced the lines further apart; this is so that you can write the meanings and the grammar (abbreviated!) under each word. See what you can do about translating this passage now!

Ἐν ἀρχῇ ἦν ὁ λόγος, καὶ ὁ λόγος ἦν πρὸς τὸν θεόν, καὶ θεὸς ἦν

ὁ λόγος. ²οὗτος ἦν ἐν ἀρχῇ πρὸς τὸν θεόν.

³πάντα δί αὐτοῦ ἐγένετο, καὶ χωρὶς αὐτοῦ ἐγένετο

οὐδὲ ἕν ὃ γέγονεν. ⁴ἐν αὐτῷ ζωὴ ἦν, καὶ ἡ ζωὴ ἦν τὸ φῶς τῶν

ἀνθρώπων, ⁵καὶ τὸ φῶς ἐν τῇ σκοτίᾳ φαίνει, καὶ ἡ

σκοτία αὐτὸ οὐ κατέλαβεν.

EXERCISES FOR
SECOND CLASS WORDS – VERBS, PAST TENSE

For each of the following words, write the tense, person, and number. Do it as in the example:

Example: ἔλυον | **tense:** imperfect | **person:** 1st | **number:** singular

ἐβαπτισάμεν

ἐδίωξεν

ἐκαλύψας

ἐλύσατε

ἐπέμπετε

ἔλυον

ἔλυσαν

ἐβαπτίσατε

ἐδιώξαμεν

ἐπείθες

ἐκαλύψεν

ἔλυες

ἐβάπτισαν

ἐβάπτιζον

ἐδιώξατε

ἐκαλύψαμεν

ἐπείσατε

ἔλυεν

ἐβάπτιζες

ἐδίωξαν

ἐδίωκον

ἐκαλύψατε

ἐβάπτιζεν

ἐδίωκες

ἐκαλύπτον

ἐκαλύψαν

ἐλύομεν

ἐβαπτίζομεν

ἐπείθεν

ἐδιώκεν

ἐκαλύπτες

ἐλύετε

ἐπέμψαμεν

ἔλυσα

ἐβαπτίζετε

ἐδιώκομεν

ἐκαλύπτεν

ἐπέμπομεν

ἔλυσας

ἐβαπτίσα

ἐδιώκετε

ἐπείσαμεν

ἐκαλύπτομεν

ἐπέμπον

ἔλυσεν

ἐβαπτίσας

ἐδιώξα

ἐκαλύπτετε

ἐπέμψας

ἐβαπτίσεν

ἐδιώξας

ἐκαλύψα

ἐλύσαμεν

ἐπέμψατε

Match the following English phrases with the appropriate Greek aorist or imperfect words:

_____	I followed	1	ὠφείλατε
_____	she followed	2	ἤρασαν
_____	we owed	3	ὑπεστρέψα
_____	she returned	4	ἐβαπτίσαμεν
_____	they baptized	5	ἠκολουθήσαμεν
_____	you (pl) returned	6	ὠφείλεν
_____	you (s) commanded	7	ἐκελεύσα
_____	I returned	8	ὑπεστρέψαμεν
_____	they returned	9	ὠφείλον
_____	they took	10	ἐκελεύσαμεν
_____	we hid	11	ἠράσαμεν
_____	she commanded	12	ἐβαπτίσαν
_____	we baptized	13	ἠκολούθησεν
_____	you (pl) commanded	14	ἐκαλύψαμεν
_____	you (s) owed	15	ἐκελεύσαν
_____	he owed	16	ἠράσατε
_____	they commanded	17	ὠφείλομεν
_____	we followed	18	ὑπεστρέψατε
_____	we took	19	ἠκολούθησα
_____	I commanded	20	ἐβαπτίσεν
_____	we returned	21	ὠφείλα
_____	you (pl) owed	22	ἠκολουθήσατε
_____	you (s) hid	23	ἐκελεύσεν
_____	he hid	24	ὑπεστρέψαν
_____	they owed	25	ὠφείλες
_____	you (pl) hid	26	ὑπεστρέψεν
_____	you (s) baptized	27	ἐβαπτίσατε
_____	I owed	28	ἤρασεν
_____	we commanded	29	ἐβαπτίσας
_____	you (s) followed	30	ἐκαλύψαν
_____	you (s) took	31	ἠκολούθησας
_____	he baptized	32	ἐκελεύσατε
_____	she took	33	ὑπεστρέψας
_____	you (pl) baptized	34	ἐκελεύσας
_____	you (pl) took	35	ἐκαλύψα
_____	I hid	36	ἤρασας
_____	they hid	37	ἐκαλύψας
_____	you (pl) followed	38	ἐκαλύψεν
_____	you (s) returned	39	ἐκαλύψατε

Translate the following sentences into English:

ὁ πιστός προφετής ἔλυεν τόν ἄλλον τέκνον.

ὁ πιστός υἱός ἐκαλύΨεν τόν μικρόν Πέτρον.

αἱ πονηραί ἐκκλησίαι ἐδιώκον τοὺς πιστούς ἀδελφούς.

ὁ ἴδιος ἀδελφή ἐδιώκεν τόν ἄλλον ἀδελφόν.

αἱ πρεσβύτεραι ἁμαρτίαι ἐδιώξαν τας ἅγιας βασιλείας.

ὁ πονηρός ἐκκλησία ἠκολούθησεν τόν ἅγιον Πέτρον.

οἱ μακάριοι ἀδελφοί ἔλυσαν ὁ καλά πλοια.

ὁ πονηρός ἄνθρωπος ἠγάπησεν τήν μικρήν ἀδελφήν.

ὁ πονηρός ὄχλος ἠκολούθησεν τόν κακόν υἱόν.

ὁ πιστός ἄνθρωπος ὤφειλεν ἄρτον ταις νεκραίς μαθηταίς.

Translate the following sentences into Greek:

God was commanding the evil crowd.

Bad hearts killed the little children.

The older sisters was sending the good bread.

Peter's house hid the holy angels.

The good disciple loved the holy life.

The other disciples commanded the last brothers.

The older child followed the other kingdom.

The holy Church saw the last witnesses.

The small children returned the blessed bread.

The bad disciples commanded the boats.

Here is John 6:22-27. By now you should be able to find all the nouns, adjectives, articles, pronouns, and verbs (present, future, imperfect, and aorist). Be sure to use the dictionary for any new words. Remember, you can figure out the grammar by looking for the distinctive endings of the declensions and conjugations. When you find them, tell the person, number, and tense for verbs, and the case, number, gender, and declension for the first-class words. Then look the word up in the dictionary and find the meaning.

²²Τῇ ἐπαύριον ὁ ὄχλος ὁ ἑστηκὼς πέραν τῆς θαλάσσης εἶδον

ὅτι πλοιάριον ἄλλο οὐκ ἦν ἐκεῖ εἰ μὴ ἕν καὶ ὅτι οὐ

συνεισῆλθεν τοῖς μαθηταῖς αὐτοῦ ὁ Ἰησοῦς εἰς τὸ πλοῖον

ἀλλὰ μόνοι οἱ μαθηταὶ αὐτοῦ ἀπῆλθον, ²³ἄλλα ἦλθεν πλοιάρια ἐκ

Τιβεριάδος ἐγγὺς τοῦ τόπου ὅπου ἔφαγον τὸν ἄρτον

εὐχαριστήσαντος τοῦ κυρίου. ²⁴ὅτε οὖν εἶδεν ὁ ὄχλος ὅτι

Ἰησοῦς οὐκ ἔστιν ἐκεῖ οὐδὲ οἱ μαθηταὶ αὐτοῦ, ἐνέβησαν

αὐτοὶ εἰς τὰ πλοιάρια καὶ ἦλθον εἰς Καφαρναοὺμ ζητοῦντες

τὸν Ἰησοῦν. ²⁵καὶ εὑρόντες αὐτὸν πέραν τῆς θαλάσσης

εἶπον αὐτῷ, ραββί, πότε ὧδε γέγονας ²⁶Ἀπεκρίθη αὐτοῖς ὁ

Ἰησοῦς καὶ εἶπεν, ἀμὴν ἀμὴν λέγω ὑμῖν, ζητεῖτέ με οὐχ ὅτι εἴδετε

σημεῖα, ἀλλ ὅτι ἐφάγετε ἐκ τῶν ἄρτων καὶ

ἐχορτάσθητε. ²⁷ἐργάζεσθε μὴ τὴν βρῶσιν τὴν ἀπολλυμένην

ἀλλὰ τὴν βρῶσιν τὴν μένουσαν εἰς ζωὴν αἰώνιον, ἣν ὁ υἱὸς

τοῦ ἀνθρώπου ὑμῖν δώσει, τοῦτον γὰρ ὁ πατὴρ ἐσφράγισεν

ὁ θεός.

EXERCISES FOR
THIRD CLASS WORDS

You should know these common adverbs, conjunctions, and prepositions. Translate each of the following words:

ἀληθῶς	τέ	ἀληθῶς	ἄρτι
ἀμήν	πρῶτον	ἀλλά	δέ
ἄνωθεν	πρός	ἀμήν	διά
ἄρτι	πάντοτε	οὐκ	εἰς
ἐκεῖ	πάλιν	οὖν	ἄρτι
νῦν	παρά	οὔτε	ἄνωθεν
ὄντως	οὔτε	παρά	ἄνωθεν
οὐδέποτε	οὖν	πάλιν	ἀληθῶς
ὅπου	οὐκ	πάντοτε	ἀμήν
οὔπω	οὐδέποτε	πρός	τέ
πάλιν	οὔπω	πρῶτον	πρῶτον
πάντοτε	ὅπου	οὐδέποτε	πρός
πρῶτον	ὄντως	οὔπω	πάντοτε
μή	νῦν	ὅπου	ἐν
οὐκ	μή	ὄντως	ἐκεῖ
ἀλλά	καί	νῦν	ἐκ
ἆρα	ἤ	μή	εἰς
γάρ	γάρ	καί	διά
δέ	ἐν	ἤ	δέ
ἤ	ἐκεῖ	γάρ	ἀλλά
καί	ἐκ	πάλιν	ἆρα
οὖν	εἰς	παρά	ἄρτι
οὔτε	διά	οὔτε	ἄνωθεν
τέ	δέ	οὖν	οὐδέποτε
ἐν	ἀμήν	οὐκ	οὔπω
παρά	ἀλλά	ἤ	ὅπου
πρός	τέ	γάρ	ὄντως
ἐκ	ἆρα	ἐν	νῦν
εἰς	ἆρα	ἐκεῖ	μή
διά	ἀληθῶς	ἐκ	καί

Translate the following phrases:

εὐχαριστέω πάντοτε

μετανοησω ἀληθῶς

οὐκ ἔσονται ἐκεῖ

ἐν τῇ συναγωγῇ

ἀλλά οὐκ ὄντως

οὔπω βαπτίζει

οὔπω πείθεις

ἡ ἀληθεία ἄνωθεν

πρῶτον λύσω

οὐδέποτε ἐπέμψεν

αμήν αμήν λέγω ὑμίν

νῦν ἐσθίσω

ἀληθῶς ἐλπίζουσιν

ὅπου εἰσίν μαθηταί?

καλύψω πάλιν

ἄνθρωποι πάντοτε ἐλπίζουσιν

οὐδέποτε πάλιν διώξουσιν

Ὅπου Πέτρον πέμψει?

ὄντως καλός ἄρτος

ὁ ἀνήρ οὔπω ἐστίν νεκρός

αὐτη ἀδελφή ἄρτι ἐστιν πρεσβυτέρια

Translate the following prepositional phrases into Greek:

in the darkness

out of the house

through the crowd

to the world

through the book

for the holy scribe

in the last boat

for the blessed angel

to the evil heart

out of heaven

into the good eye

through the son

through work

into the kingdom

out of love

to the righteous sister

for glory

in the beginning

into the faithful church

to the small child

for the prophet

in honor of the dead prophet

out of the law

through Christ

for Peter

out of the last word

Translate the following sentences into English:

οἱ πονηροί ἄνθρωποι πάλιν ἐδιώξαν τήν πιστάν ἐκκλησίαν.

ὁ πονηρός ἀνήρ ἔγραψεν πρός τήν ἐκκλησίαν, δέ ἡ ἐκκλησία ἠκολύθησαν Ἰησούν.

τά καλά τέκνα πάντοτε ἀγαπούσιν ὁ δίκαια ἔργα .

οἱ δίκαιοι μαθηταί ἐβαπτίσεν τάς ἀδελφάς πρῶτον.

τά μικρά τέκνα ἐκαλύψεν ἐν μικροῖς πλοῖοις, ἆρα πονηροί ἄνθρωποι οὐκ ἐβλέψαν τά τέκνα.

ὁ πιστός ἄγγελος ἐπέμψεν τόν προφήτην, ἀλλά ὁ ὄχλος ἐδιώξεν τόν ἀνδρά.

ὁ ὄχλος ἀπέκτειναν τάς δίκαιας ἀδελφάς, και οὐδέποτε μετενόησαν.

Ἐκεῖ, ἐν τη ἐκκλησία, οἱ μαθηταί ἠκολούθησαν τούς καλούς γραμματεάς.

αἱ ἔσχαται μαρτυρίαι ἠλπίσαν, οὖν εὐχαρίσησαν πρός Θεόν.

τόν κακόν νόμον ἄξει πρός τήν κακήν ζωήν.

Translate the following sentences into Greek:

The holy disciples wrote to the other witnesses.

The holy children will see blessed Jesus.

James hid the prophet, but the crowd saw and persecuted him.

Righteous words are from above, out of Heaven.

The good brothers wrote to the churches and to Peter.

The Lord preached to the other disciples.

The blessed witnesses will see the glory of God in Christ.

Christ will command the prophets from Heaven.

The boats were sufficient, and the disciples hid from the scribes.

The brothers repented, and were baptized, in Christ.

Here is John 6:22-27 again. See if you can find all the adverbs, negatives, prepositions, and conjunctions. Be sure to use the dictionary for any new words. Don't let the endings confuse you this time; sometimes an adverb in particular will have the same ending as a noun or verb does – the only way to avoid that is to know the word's meaning. For every preposition, find the case of the noun that is its object.

²²Τῇ ἐπαύριον ὁ ὄχλος ὁ ἑστηκὼς πέραν τῆς θαλάσσης εἶδον

ὅτι πλοιάριον ἄλλο οὐκ ἦν ἐκεῖ εἰ μὴ ἕν καὶ ὅτι οὐ

συνεισῆλθεν τοῖς μαθηταῖς αὐτοῦ ὁ Ἰησοῦς εἰς τὸ πλοῖον

ἀλλὰ μόνοι οἱ μαθηταὶ αὐτοῦ ἀπῆλθον, ²³ἄλλα ἦλθεν πλοιάρια ἐκ

Τιβεριάδος ἐγγὺς τοῦ τόπου ὅπου ἔφαγον τὸν ἄρτον

εὐχαριστήσαντος τοῦ κυρίου. ²⁴ὅτε οὖν εἶδεν ὁ ὄχλος ὅτι

Ἰησοῦς οὐκ ἔστιν ἐκεῖ οὐδὲ οἱ μαθηταὶ αὐτοῦ, ἐνέβησαν

αὐτοὶ εἰς τὰ πλοιάρια καὶ ἦλθον εἰς Καφαρναοὺμ ζητοῦντες

τὸν Ἰησοῦν. ²⁵καὶ εὑρόντες αὐτὸν πέραν τῆς θαλάσσης

εἶπον αὐτῷ, ραββί, πότε ὧδε γέγονας ²⁶Ἀπεκρίθη αὐτοῖς ὁ

Ἰησοῦς καὶ εἶπεν, ἀμὴν ἀμὴν λέγω ὑμῖν, ζητεῖτέ με οὐχ ὅτι εἴδετε

σημεῖα, ἀλλ ὅτι ἐφάγετε ἐκ τῶν ἄρτων καὶ

ἐχορτάσθητε. ²⁷ἐργάζεσθε μὴ τὴν βρῶσιν τὴν ἀπολλυμένην

ἀλλὰ τὴν βρῶσιν τὴν μένουσαν εἰς ζωὴν αἰώνιον, ἣν ὁ υἱὸς

τοῦ ἀνθρώπου ὑμῖν δώσει, τοῦτον γὰρ ὁ πατὴρ ἐσφράγισεν

ὁ θεός.

EXERCISES FOR
FIRST CLASS WORDS – NOUNS

For each of the following words, write the stem, the ending, and the meaning. Do it as in the example:

Example:

Word: λύομαι	stem: λυ-	ending: -ομαι	meaning: I am being loosed
βλέπεσθε			
καλύπτονται			
πέμπεται			
ἐγείρεσθε			
καλύπτῃ			
καλυπτόμεθα			
πείθομεθα			
βλέπεται			
ὀφείλεται			
ὀφείλονται			
πείθῃ			
ἐγείρεται			
πέμπομαι			
πεμπόμεθα			
πέμπονται			
βλέπομαι			
βλέπονται			
καλύπτεται			
ἐγείρομαι			
ἐγείρονται			
πείθεσθε			
πείθομαι			
βλεπόμεθα			
καλύπτεσθε			
ὀφειλόμεθα			
πέμπεσθε			
ἐγειρόμεθα			
πείθεται			
πέμπῃ			
βλέπῃ			
καλύπτομαι			
οφείλη			
ἐγείρῃ			
ὀφείλεσθε			
πείθονται			

For each of the following words, write the stem, the ending, and the meaning.

Word: λύσομαι	stem: λυ-	ending: -ομαι	meaning: I will be loosed
ἐκαλυψάμεθα			
ἐπείσω			
πέμψονται			
ἐβλέψσμην			
ἐγείρσομαι			
ἐκαλύψασθε			
ἐπείσατο			
ἐβλέψω			
ἐγείρσῃ			
ἐκαλύψαντο			
ἐπεισάμεθα			
ἐβλέψατο			
ἐγείρσεται			
ἐπείσασθε			
ὀφείλσομαι			
ἐβλεψάμεθα			
ἐγειρσόμεθα			
ἐπείσαντο			
ὀφείλσῃ			
ἐβλέψασθε			
ἐγείρσεσθε			
ὀφείλσεται			
πέμψομαι			
ἐβλέψαντο			
ἐγείρσονται			
ὀφειλσόμεθα			
πέμψῃ			
ἐκαλύψαμην			
ὀφείλσεσθε			
πέμψεται			
ἐκαλύψω			
ὀφείλσονται			
πεμψόμεθα			
ἐκαλύψατο			
ἐπείσαμην			
πέμψεσθε			

Translate the following phrases into Greek, using the appropriate personal pronoun with the phrase:

Example: I loosed – ἐγώ ἔλυσα

she sent it to them
they will say it
we wrote to you
I owe it to them
I preached
it has
you (pl) will preach
He will judge me
you will command him
he has it
I love him
the man tempted him
you (pl) hid in the house
she returned to him
they hope in him
we will give thanks
you will see
he led them
I baptize you
we baptize
you will repent
he wishes
she persuaded them
you (pl) will eat it
you will follow me
he killed her
I owe you
it sends us
they gave thanks
she said to them
they will persuade you
we follow
he ate it
it was loosed
you (pl) said to me

Translate the following sentences into English:

οἱ δίκαιοι διδάσκαλοι ἐκαλύψαντο ἐν τῇ συναγωγῃ.

Οἱ ἄνθρωποι ὑποστρέψουσιν τάς βασιλείας πρός μαθητάς Ἰουδαίους.

αἵ ἔσχαται μαρτυρίαι ἐπέμψαντο πρός τούς ἔσχατους προφέτας.

οἵ γραμματές Ἰουδαίοι ἐκάλυψεν ἐν τῷ ἱερῳ, δέ ἄνθρωποι πονηροί ἐδιώξαν αὐτούς.

ἡ ἀδελφή ἐσθίεν τόν ἄρτον και ἐχαίρεν.

ὁ καλός μαθητής ἔλεξεν λόγον ἅγιον πρός τόν ὄχλον.

οἱ Ἰουδαίοι διδάσκαλοι ἤρθονται πρός τάς συναγωγάς.

ὁ δίκαιος προφετής ἐχαίρσεν ἐν τῇ μαρτυρίᾳ τέκνων.

Τό ὄνομα Χριστοῦ ἐστίν πάλιν τιμή πρός τέκνα αὐτά.

Οἱ πλοῖοι μαθητῶν ἠγείρθοντα ἐν τῇ θάλασσῃ.

Translate the following sentences into Greek:

The bad men will hide in the small house.

Life in the other world will follow a righteous life in God's church.

The happy church is where the bread of life is eaten.

The righteous angels will send the disciples to other fields of work.

The holy child was baptized in the church by the faithful prophets.

The sinful disciple was following the truth, and then he repented.

The good brother hid himself and his books in the church.

The sinful churches were sending evil men in boats on the sea.

The holy sisters were persuaded by the witnesses of Christ.

The faithful disciples were led by Jesus to the blessed glories of Heaven.

Here is John 6:22-27 again. See if you can find the middle and passive forms for verbs. Be sure to use the dictionary for any new words. Remember, go by the ending to determine which is middle/passive. Then do your best to translate this passage.

²²Τῇ ἐπαύριον ὁ ὄχλος ὁ ἑστηκὼς πέραν τῆς θαλάσσης εἶδον

ὅτι πλοιάριον ἄλλο οὐκ ἦν ἐκεῖ εἰ μὴ ἕν καὶ ὅτι οὐ

συνεισῆλθεν τοῖς μαθηταῖς αὐτοῦ ὁ Ἰησοῦς εἰς τὸ πλοῖον

ἀλλὰ μόνοι οἱ μαθηταὶ αὐτοῦ ἀπῆλθον, ²³ἄλλα ἦλθεν πλοιάρια ἐκ

Τιβεριάδος ἐγγὺς τοῦ τόπου ὅπου ἔφαγον τὸν ἄρτον

εὐχαριστήσαντος τοῦ κυρίου. ²⁴ὅτε οὖν εἶδεν ὁ ὄχλος ὅτι

Ἰησοῦς οὐκ ἔστιν ἐκεῖ οὐδὲ οἱ μαθηταὶ αὐτοῦ, ἐνέβησαν

αὐτοὶ εἰς τὰ πλοιάρια καὶ ἦλθον εἰς Καφαρναοὺμ ζητοῦντες

τὸν Ἰησοῦν. ²⁵καὶ εὑρόντες αὐτὸν πέραν τῆς θαλάσσης

εἶπον αὐτῷ, ραββί, πότε ὧδε γέγονας ²⁶Ἀπεκρίθη αὐτοῖς ὁ

Ἰησοῦς καὶ εἶπεν, ἀμὴν ἀμὴν λέγω ὑμῖν, ζητεῖτέ με οὐχ ὅτι εἴδετε

σημεῖα, ἀλλ ὅτι ἐφάγετε ἐκ τῶν ἄρτων καὶ

ἐχορτάσθητε. ²⁷ἐργάζεσθε μὴ τὴν βρῶσιν τὴν ἀπολλυμένην

ἀλλὰ τὴν βρῶσιν τὴν μένουσαν εἰς ζωὴν αἰώνιον, ἣν ὁ υἱὸς

τοῦ ἀνθρώπου ὑμῖν δώσει, τοῦτον γὰρ ὁ πατὴρ ἐσφράγισεν

ὁ θεός.

EXERCISES FOR
THIRD DECLENSION & PREPOSITIONS

For each of the following words, write the stem, the ending, and the meaning. Do it as in the example:

Example:

σαρκος   **stem:** σαρκ-   **ending:** -ος   **meaning:** of flesh

χάρισιν	γυναικές
δαίμονος	νύξ
ἐλπίδα	πατρί
φωτές	σώματες
νυκτῶν	σώτρας
πατράς	χάριστι
σώτρι	δαίμονας
χάριστας	φῶς
δαίμονι	γυναικῶν
ἐλπίδες	νυκτός
φωτῶν	πατρά
γυνή	σώμασιν
νυξίν	χάριστα
σώμα	ἐλπίς
σώτρα	φωτός
δαίμονα	γυναιξίν
ἐλπίδων	νυκτί
φωσίν	πατρές
γυναικός	σώματας
νυκτάς	χάριστες
σώματος	ἐλπίδος
σώτρες	φωτί
δαίμονες	γυναικάς
ἐλπίσιν	νυκτά
φωτάς	πατρών
γυναικί	σώτηρ
πατήρ	χάριστων
σώματι	δαίμων
σώτρων	ἐλπίδι
χάρις	φωτά
δαίμονων	νυκτές
ἐλπίδας	πατρίσιν
γυναικά	σώτρος
πατρός	ὕδατος
σώματα	
σώσιν	
χάριστος	
δαίμουσιν	

Translate the following phrases into Greek:

to the evil demon

of the holy Savior

in the good light

of God's grace

under the waters

into the last hope

out of the older garments

down to the small fish

into the other villages

from bad nights

through the faithful father

in the Holy Spirit

through sinful flesh

above the Jewish soldiers

out of the body

through the grace of God

from the demon of death

to the blessed Savior

into good light

through the grace of Christ

above the waters

into a small garment

alongside the small fish

from the small villages

in a holy night

through the Jewish father

through the Spirit of a righteous God

under dead flesh

to God's own soldiers

up to the faithful church

Give the appropriate Greek translation in each blank:

God saw the children _____ (in the night).

_____ (The father) of the woman was a scribe.

I suffered because of the persecution _____ (of the wicked soldiers).

_____ (The Holy Spirit) fights against _____ (the flesh).

We are born _____ (of water) and _____ (of the Spirit).

The farmers went _____ (into the little village).

We are born _____ (out of the world) and _____ (into the grace of God).

Soldiers carried _____ (the dead body) _____ (into the synagogue).

They _____ (were walking) _____ (in the light of day).

Our hope is _____ (in Christ the Savior), our _____ (hope of glory).

_____ (Fish in the sea) are for eating.

The designs _____ (on the garments) were colorful.

Christ is _____ (above the evil demons).

Christ _____ (will take us into heaven).

The disciples _____ (asked) a favor _____ (of the women).

Walk _____ (in the light of truth) and _____ _____ (alongside Jesus).

Translate the following sentences into English:

οἱ πιστοί γραμματές ἦρεν ὀνόματα τῶν μαθητῶν καί εὐχαρίστησεν Θεῷ.

οἱ ἄνθρωποι ἠσθίεν κακούς ἰχθούς, καί αὐτό ἠποκτείνεν αὐτούς.

αἱ μικραί κῶμαι ἐκαλύψεν τούς πιστούς μαθητάς ἀπό στρατιώτων πονηρῶν.

οἱ πρεσβύτεροι ἄνθρωποι ἦξεν μικρά τέκνα εἰς νυκτί.

οἱ ἔσχατοι πατρῶν ἀποκτείσουσιν ἐν τῷ ἱερῷ.

τό ἅγιον πνεῦμα ἔκρινεν καρδίας πονηρῶν ἀνθρῶπων.

αἱ ἀλλαί γύναι ἐπέμψουσιν τόν ἄρτον αὐτοίς τέκνοις ἐν τῇ κωμη.

αἱ μητρές πάλιν ἐγείρξουσιν αὐτά τέκνα Ἰουδαία ἐν τῷ βιβλίῳ Θεοῦ.

ὁ Θεός οὐρανοῦ οὐδέποτε διώξει αὐτα τέκνα.

οἱ ἄνθρωποι τῶν ἁμαρτωλῶν ὀφθάλμων ἐβλέψουσιν τόν ἔργον δαίμωνος, δε αυτοί οὐκ μετενόησεν ἐκ αὐτῶν ἁμαρτίων.

Translate the following sentences into Greek:

The evil children were walking into the small village.

The small church was eating the bread of life, but soldiers persecuted them.

The Jewish sister returned the bad fish to the scribes in the synagogue.

The last of the soldiers persecuted the faithful disciples.

The bad men will never persuade the faithful brothers.

The evil woman rejoiced in the sinful work of demons.

Now we will give thanks for the truths of God in the book.

The angels were commanding the seas, and so the men in the boats repented.

The evil men persuaded the kingdoms of the world; so they did not repent.

The sinful world rejoiced in evil works, but God will kill it.

Here is John 21:1-14. By now you can pretty much analyze the basic parts of speech, especially in a section like this which is mostly narrative. Find all the first class words (giving the details of each) and the third class words. Then locate the verbs and give the details for them (don't worry about the verb types that you haven't studied yet). Then give a stab at translating the passage. Don't worry, we'll be working on this passage for the next few lessons!

Μετὰ ταῦτα ἐφανέρωσεν ἑαυτὸν πάλιν ὁ Ἰησοῦς τοῖς

μαθηταῖς ἐπὶ τῆς θαλάσσης τῆς Τιβεριάδος, ἐφανέρωσεν δὲ

οὕτως. ²ἦσαν ὁμοῦ Σίμων Πέτρος καὶ Θωμᾶς ὁ λεγόμενος

Δίδυμος καὶ Ναθαναὴλ ὁ ἀπὸ Κανὰ τῆς Γαλιλαίας καὶ οἱ τοῦ Ζεβεδαίου

καὶ ἄλλοι ἐκ τῶν μαθητῶν αὐτοῦ δύο. ³λέγει αὐτοῖς Σίμων Πέτρος,

ὑπάγω ἁλιεύειν. λέγουσιν αὐτῷ, ἐρχόμεθα καὶ ἡμεῖς σὺν σοί. ἐξῆλθον

καὶ ἐνέβησαν εἰς τὸ πλοῖον, καὶ ἐν ἐκείνῃ τῇ νυκτὶ ἐπίασαν οὐδέν.

⁴πρωΐας δὲ ἤδη γενομένης ἔστη Ἰησοῦς εἰς τὸν αἰγιαλόν, οὐ μέντοι ᾔδ

εισαν οἱ μαθηταὶ ὅτι Ἰησοῦς ἐστιν. ⁵λέγει οὖν αὐτοῖς ὁ Ἰησοῦς,

παιδία, μή τι προσφάγιον ἔχετε ἀπεκρίθησαν αὐτῷ, οὔ. ⁶ὁ δὲ εἶπεν

αὐτοῖς, βάλετε εἰς τὰ δεξιὰ μέρη τοῦ πλοίου τὸ δίκτυον, καὶ

εὑρήσετε. ἔβαλον οὖν, καὶ οὐκέτι αὐτὸ ἑλκύσαι ἴσχυον ἀπὸ

τοῦ πλήθους τῶν ἰχθύων. ⁷λέγει οὖν ὁ μαθητὴς ἐκεῖνος ὃν

ἠγάπα ὁ Ἰησοῦς τῷ Πέτρῳ, ὁ κύριος ἐστιν. Σίμων οὖν

Πέτρος ἀκούσας ὅτι ὁ κύριος ἐστιν τὸν ἐπενδύτην

διεζώσατο, ἦν γὰρ γυμνός, καὶ ἔβαλεν ἑαυτὸν εἰς τὴν

θάλασσαν, [8]οἱ δὲ ἄλλοι μαθηταὶ τῷ πλοιαρίῳ ἦλθον, οὐ γὰρ

ἦσαν μακρὰν ἀπὸ τῆς γῆς ἀλλὰ ὡς ἀπὸ πηχῶν διακοσίων,

σύροντες τὸ δίκτυον τῶν ἰχθύων. [9]ὡς οὖν ἀπέβησαν εἰς τὴν

γῆν βλέπουσιν ἀνθρακιὰν κειμένην καὶ ὀψάριον ἐπικείμενον

καὶ ἄρτον. [10]λέγει αὐτοῖς ὁ Ἰησοῦς, ἐνέγκατε ἀπὸ τῶν

ὀψαρίων ὧν ἐπιάσατε νῦν. [11]ἀνέβη οὖν Σίμων Πέτρος καὶ

εἵλκυσεν τὸ δίκτυον εἰς τὴν γῆν μεστὸν ἰχθύων μεγάλων

ἑκατὸν πεντήκοντα τριῶν, καὶ τοσούτων ὄντων οὐκ ἐσχίσθη

τὸ δίκτυον. [12]λέγει αὐτοῖς ὁ Ἰησοῦς, δεῦτε ἀριστήσατε.

οὐδεὶς δὲ ἐτόλμα τῶν μαθητῶν ἐξετάσαι αὐτόν, σὺ τίς εἶ

εἰδότες ὅτι ὁ κύριος ἐστιν. [13]ἔρχεται Ἰησοῦς καὶ λαμβάνει

τὸν ἄρτον καὶ δίδωσιν αὐτοῖς, καὶ τὸ ὀψάριον ὁμοίως. [14]τοῦτο ἤδη

τρίτον ἐφανερώθη Ἰησοῦς τοῖς μαθηταῖς ἐγερθεὶς ἐκ

νεκρῶν.

EXERCISES FOR
SECOND CLASS WORDS – SUBJUNCTIVE MOOD

For each of the following words, write the stem, the person, the number, the tense, and the meaning. Do it as in the example:

Example:

	stem:	person:	number:	tense:	meaning:
λύσω	λυ-	1st	s.	aorist	I might have loosed
ἀκούσῃ					
διδάσκῃς					
διδάξωσιν					
σώσητε					
ἀκούωμεν					
διδάξῃ					
πιστεύῃς					
σώσωσιν					
ἀκούητε					
πιστεύσῃ					
πιστεύσῃς					
διδάξητε					
πιστεῦσῃ					
πιστεύσωμεν					
διδάσκῃς					
διδάξωσιν					
πιστεύητε					
πιστεύσωμεν					
διδάξῃ					
πιστεύητε					
πιστεύσωσιν					
σώσῃς					
διδάξωμεν					
πιστεύσωσιν					
σώσῃ					
ἀκούῃς					
διδάξητε					
σώζωμεν					

Translate the following phrases into Greek, the left column in present subjunctive, and the right column in aorist subjunctive:

in order that we might believe	so that they might preach
so that I might go	so that we might pray
in order that she might find	in order that he might save
in order that we would not die	so that we might be able
in order that it might remain	in order that you (s) might answer
in order that he might teach	so that he would die
so that he might hear	so that she would believe
in order that you (pl) might say	in order that we would open
so that he might open	in order that he might hear
in order that we might answer	in order that they might pity
in order that we might pity	in order that we might go
so that you (s) might pray	so that it might find
so that we might be able	in order that he might send

Another use for the subjunctive is in "if-then" situations. For example, you can have a sentence like this:

ἐὰν μείνητε ἐν ἐμοὶ καὶ τὰ ῥήματα μου ἐν ὑμῖν μείνῃ ...

Translated, it reads thus:

If you remain in me and my words remain in you, (then) ... (John 15:7)

The μείνητε and the μείνῃ are subjunctive verbs.

Underline the subjunctive verbs in the following sentences and translate:

ἐάν ἐσθίωμεν τόν ἄρτον, ἀποθνήξομεν.

ἐάν ὁ μαθητής κηρύσσῃ, πιστεύσομεν τόν εὐαγγέλιον.

ἐάν ὁ ἀνήρ μενῃ ἐν τῇ φυλακῇ, πάξει.

ἐάν Θεός ἀποκρίνηται τόν ἄρχα, ἀκοῦσει.

ἐάν εὑρίσκῃς τόν Χριστόν, χαίρησῃ.

ἐάν διδάσκητε τούς μαθητάς, ἔστε καλά τέκνα Θεοῦ.

ἐάν ὁ Πέτρος βλέψῃ τόν Ἰάκωβον, ἀποστέλει αὐτόν πρός τήν ἐκκλησίαν.

Translate the following sentences into English:

There are two subjunctives in the following verse.

οὕτως γὰρ ἠγάπησεν ὁ θεὸς τὸν κόσμον, ὥστε τὸν υἱὸν τὸν μονογενῆ ἔδωκεν, ἵνα πᾶς ὁ πιστεύων εἰς αὐτὸν μὴ ἀπόληται ἀλλ ἔχῃ ζωὴν αἰώνιον. (John 3:16)

There is one subjunctive in the following verse.

ἐὰν οὖν ὁ υἱὸς ὑμᾶς ἐλευθερώσῃ, ὄντως ἐλεύθεροι ἔσεσθε. (John 8:36)

There are two subjunctives in the following verse.

Ἀμὴν λέγω ὑμῖν, ὅσα ἐὰν δήσητε ἐπὶ τῆς γῆς ἔσται δεδεμένα ἐν οὐρανῷ, καὶ ὅσα ἐὰν λύσητε ἐπὶ τῆς γῆς ἔσται λελυμένα ἐν οὐρανῷ. (Matthew 18:18)

There are two subjunctives in the following verse.

Καὶ ἔρχεται εἷς τῶν ἀρχισυναγώγων, ὀνόματι Ἰάϊρος, καὶ ἰδὼν αὐτὸν πίπτει πρὸς τοὺς πόδας αὐτοῦ ²³καὶ παρακαλεῖ αὐτὸν πολλὰ λέγων ὅτι τὸ θυγάτριον μου ἐσχάτως ἔχει, ἵνα ἐλθὼν ἐπιθῇς τὰς χεῖρας αὐτῇ ἵνα σωθῇ καὶ ζήσῃ. (Mark 5:22-23)

There are two subjunctives in the following verse.

ὃς ἐὰν ζητήσῃ τὴν ψυχὴν αὐτοῦ περιποιήσασθαι ἀπολέσει αὐτήν, ὃς δ ἂν ἀπολέσῃ ζωογονήσει αὐτήν. (Luke 17:33)

Translate the following sentences into Greek:

The disciples prayed in order that they might hear the Word of God.

The ruler commanded the people so that they might open their hearts to him.

You will find the truth of Christ blessed, that you might live and not die.

The Pharisee and the scribe didn't believe in Christ; they were not able to believe (*infinitive form* – πιστευσαι) in him.

Peter preached the gospel in order that the people might open their hearts to the Holy Spirit.

We will remain here in order that we might eat with the sisters.

The soldier remained in the prison so that he might persecute Peter.

I will send the bread that the brothers gave to me.

Jesus answered the disciples so that they might hear the words of God.

Jesus opened his heart to us so that we might believe in him.

Here is John 21:1-14 again. Keep working!

Μετὰ ταῦτα ἐφανέρωσεν ἑαυ‐ὸν πάλιν ὁ Ἰησοῦς τοῖς

μαθηταῖς ἐπὶ τῆς θαλάσσης τῆς Τιβεριάδος, ἐφανέρωσεν δὲ

οὕτως. ²ἦσαν ὁμοῦ Σίμων Πέτρος καὶ Θωμᾶς ὁ λεγόμενος

Δίδυμος καὶ Ναθαναὴλ ὁ ἀπὸ Κανὰ τῆς Γαλιλαίας καὶ οἱ τοῦ Ζεβεδαίου

καὶ ἄλλοι ἐκ τῶν μαθητῶν αὐτοῦ δύο. ³λέγει αὐτοῖς Σίμων Πέτρος,

ὑπάγω ἁλιεύειν. λέγουσιν αὐτῷ, ἐρχόμεθα καὶ ἡμεῖς σὺν σοί. ἐξῆλθον

καὶ ἐνέβησαν εἰς τὸ πλοῖον, καὶ ἐν ἐκείνῃ τῇ νυκτὶ ἐπίασαν οὐδέν.

⁴πρωΐας δὲ ἤδη γενομένης ἔστη Ἰησοῦς εἰς τὸν αἰγιαλόν, οὐ μέντοι ᾔδ

εισαν οἱ μαθηταὶ ὅτι Ἰησοῦς ἐστιν. ⁵λέγει οὖν αὐτοῖς ὁ Ἰησοῦς,

παιδία, μή τι προσφάγιον ἔχετε ἀπεκρίθησαν αὐτῷ, οὔ. ⁶ὁ δὲ εἶπεν

αὐτοῖς, βάλετε εἰς τὰ δεξιὰ μέρη τοῦ πλοίου τὸ δίκτυον, καὶ

εὑρήσετε. ἔβαλον οὖν, καὶ οὐκέτι αὐτὸ ἑλκύσαι ἴσχυον ἀπὸ

τοῦ πλήθους τῶν ἰχθύων. ⁷λέγει οὖν ὁ μαθητὴς ἐκεῖνος ὃν

ἠγάπα ὁ Ἰησοῦς τῷ Πέτρῳ, ὁ κύριος ἐστιν. Σίμων οὖν

Πέτρος ἀκούσας ὅτι ὁ κύριος ἐστιν τὸν ἐπενδύτην

διεζώσατο, ἦν γὰρ γυμνός, καὶ ἔβαλεν ἑαυτὸν εἰς τὴν

θάλασσαν, ⁸οἱ δὲ ἄλλοι μαθηταὶ τῷ πλοιαρίῳ ἦλθον, οὐ γὰρ

ἦσαν μακρὰν ἀπὸ τῆς γῆς ἀλλὰ ὡς ἀπὸ πηχῶν διακοσίων,

σύροντες τὸ δίκτυον τῶν ἰχθύων. ⁹ὡς οὖν ἀπέβησαν εἰς τὴν

γῆν βλέπουσιν ἀνθρακιὰν κειμένην καὶ ὀψάριον ἐπικείμενον

καὶ ἄρτον. ¹⁰λέγει αὐτοῖς ὁ Ἰησοῦς, ἐνέγκατε ἀπὸ τῶν

ὀψαρίων ὧν ἐπιάσατε νῦν. ¹¹ἀνέβη οὖν Σίμων Πέτρος καὶ

εἵλκυσεν τὸ δίκτυον εἰς τὴν γῆν μεστὸν ἰχθύων μεγάλων

ἑκατὸν πεντήκοντα τριῶν, καὶ τοσούτων ὄντων οὐκ ἐσχίσθη

τὸ δίκτυον. ¹²λέγει αὐτοῖς ὁ Ἰησοῦς, δεῦτε ἀριστήσατε.

οὐδεὶς δὲ ἐτόλμα τῶν μαθητῶν ἐξετάσαι αὐτόν, σὺ τίς εἶ

εἰδότες ὅτι ὁ κύριος ἐστιν. ¹³ἔρχεται Ἰησοῦς καὶ λαμβάνει

τὸν ἄρτον καὶ δίδωσιν αὐτοῖς, καὶ τὸ ὀψάριον ὁμοίως. ¹⁴τοῦτο ἤδη

τρίτον ἐφανερώθη Ἰησοῦς τοῖς μαθηταῖς ἐγερθεὶς ἐκ

νεκρῶν.

EXERCISES FOR
SECOND CLASS WORDS – PERFECT & PLUPERFECT

For each of the following words, write the stem, person, number, tense, and meaning. Do it as in the example:
Example:

	stem:	person:	number:	tense:	meaning:
λέλυσα	λυ-	1st	s.	perfect	I have loosed
βεβάπτικα					
ἔγνωκει					
ἔγνωκεν					
πεφανέρωκα					
πεποιήκειτε					
βεβάπτικας					
ἐγνώκειμεν					
πεφανέρωκας					
πεποιήκεισαν					
βεβάπτικεν					
ἔγνωκεις					
ἔγνωκατε					
τετήρηκα					
βεβαπτίκαμεν					
ἐγνώκεισιν					
ἐγνώκασιν					
πεφανερώκαμεν					
τετήρηκας					
βεβαπτίκατε					
πεφανερώκατε					
πεποιήκειν					
τετήρηκεν					
βεβαπτίκασιν					
πεφανερώκασιν					
πεποιήκεις					
τετηρήκαμεν					
ἐγνώκειτε					
ἔγνωκα					
πεποιήκει					
τετηρήκατε					
ἔγνωκειν					
ἔγνωκας					
πεποιήκειμεν					
τετηρήκασιν					

Translate the following phrases into Greek, the left column in perfect tense, and the right column in pluperfect tense:

you (s) have baptized	he had fulfilled
she has done	we had revealed
he has given	I had begotten
they have revealed	you (pl) had baptized
we have kept	she had known
I have sought	they had given
you (pl) have given	it had done
he has begotten	we had sought
we have known	I had revealed
you (s) have begotten	we had baptized
we have given	you (s) had known
I have fulfilled	they had sought
he has kept	we had done

Translate the following sentences into Greek:

Christ had baptized the disciples.

I have done the work of the Father.

Peter had revealed the truth to James.

The sisters had sought Jesus in the synagogue.

We have known the truth of God.

The hand of God has given us the food.

The prophets had revealed salvation to us.

The power of the Spirit has begotten the son of God.

God has fulfilled his truth in the land.

The Pharisees have not kept the word of God.

Peter had not known the power of Christ.

The child has given the gift to his brother.

But his brother had not kept the gift.

Translate the following sentences into English (hint: they have perfect verbs in them!):

καὶ οὐδεὶς ἀναβέβηκεν εἰς τὸν οὐρανὸν εἰ μὴ ὁ ἐκ τοῦ οὐρανοῦ καταβάς, ὁ υἱὸς τοῦ ἀνθρώπου. (John 3:13)

ἐγὼ ἐλήλυθα ἐν τῷ ὀνόματι τοῦ πατρός μου, καὶ οὐ λαμβάνετέ με, (John 5:43)

Ἀλλ εἶπον ὑμῖν ὅτι καὶ ἑωράκατέ ⸰με καὶ οὐ πιστεύετε. (John 6:36)

οὐχ ὅτι τὸν πατέρα ἑώρακέν τις εἰ μὴ ὁ ὢν παρὰ τοῦ θεοῦ, οὗτος ἑώρακεν τὸν πατέρα. (John 6:46)

τὰ ῥήματα ἃ ἐγὼ λελάληκα ὑμῖν πνεῦμά ἐστιν καὶ ζωή ἐστιν. (John 6:63)

ταῦτα λελάληκα ὑμῖν ἵνα ἐν ἐμοὶ εἰρήνην ἔχητε. ἐν τῷ κόσμῳ θλῖψιν ἔχετε, ἀλλὰ θαρσεῖτε, ἐγὼ νενίκηκα τὸν κόσμον. (John 16:33)

Here is John 21:1-14 one last time. By now you ought to be pretty close to getting it completed.

Μετὰ ταῦτα ἐφανέρωσεν ἑαυτὸν πάλιν ὁ Ἰησοῦς τοῖς

μαθηταῖς ἐπὶ τῆς θαλάσσης τῆς Τιβεριάδος, ἐφανέρωσεν δὲ

οὕτως. ²ἦσαν ὁμοῦ Σίμων Πέτρος καὶ Θωμᾶς ὁ λεγόμενος

Δίδυμος καὶ Ναθαναὴλ ὁ ἀπὸ Κανὰ τῆς Γαλιλαίας καὶ οἱ τοῦ Ζεβεδαίου

καὶ ἄλλοι ἐκ τῶν μαθητῶν αὐτοῦ δύο. ³λέγει αὐτοῖς Σίμων Πέτρος,

ὑπάγω ἁλιεύειν. λέγουσιν αὐτῷ. ἐρχόμεθα καὶ ἡμεῖς σὺν σοί. ἐξῆλθον

καὶ ἐνέβησαν εἰς τὸ πλοῖον, καὶ ἐν ἐκείνῃ τῇ νυκτὶ ἐπίασαν οὐδέν.

⁴πρωί ας δὲ ἤδη γενομένης ἔστη Ἰησοῦς εἰς τὸν αἰγιαλόν, οὐ μέντοι ᾔδ

εισαν οἱ μαθηταὶ ὅτι Ἰησοῦς ἐστιν. ⁵λέγει οὖν αὐτοῖς ὁ Ἰησοῦς,

παιδία, μή τι προσφάγιον ἔχετε ἀπεκρίθησαν αὐτῷ, οὔ. ⁶ὁ δὲ εἶπεν

αὐτοῖς, βάλετε εἰς τὰ δεξιὰ μέρη τοῦ πλοίου τὸ δίκτυον, καὶ

εὑρήσετε. ἔβαλον οὖν, καὶ οἰκέτι αὐτὸ ἑλκύσαι ἴσχυον ἀπὸ

τοῦ πλήθους τῶν ἰχθύων. ⁷λέγει οὖν ὁ μαθητὴς ἐκεῖνος ὃν

ἠγάπα ὁ Ἰησοῦς τῷ Πέτρῳ, ὁ κύριος ἐστιν. Σίμων οὖν

Πέτρος ἀκούσας ὅτι ὁ κύριος ἐστιν τὸν ἐπενδύτην

διεζώσατο, ἦν γὰρ γυμνός, καὶ ἔβαλεν ἑαυτὸν εἰς τὴν θάλασσαν, [8]οἱ δὲ ἄλλοι μαθηταὶ τῷ πλοιαρίῳ ἦλθον, οὐ γὰρ ἦσαν μακρὰν ἀπὸ τῆς γῆς ἀλλὰ ὡς ἀπὸ πηχῶν διακοσίων, σύροντες τὸ δίκτυον τῶν ἰχθύων. [9]ὡς οὖν ἀπέβησαν εἰς τὴν γῆν βλέπουσιν ἀνθρακιὰν κειμένην καὶ ὀψάριον ἐπικείμενον καὶ ἄρτον. [10]λέγει αὐτοῖς ὁ Ἰησοῦς, ἐνέγκατε ἀπὸ τῶν ὀψαρίων ὧν ἐπιάσατε νῦν. [11]ἀνέβη οὖν Σίμων Πέτρος καὶ εἵλκυσεν τὸ δίκτυον εἰς τὴν γῆν μεστὸν ἰχθύων μεγάλων ἑκατὸν πεντήκοντα τριῶν, καὶ τοσούτων ὄντων οὐκ ἐσχίσθη τὸ δίκτυον. [12]λέγει αὐτοῖς ὁ Ἰησοῦς, δεῦτε ἀριστήσατε. οὐδεὶς δὲ ἐτόλμα τῶν μαθητῶν ἐξετάσαι αὐτόν, σὺ τίς εἶ εἰδότες ὅτι ὁ κύριός ἐστιν. [13]ἔρχεται Ἰησοῦς καὶ λαμβάνει τὸν ἄρτον καὶ δίδωσιν αὐτοῖς, καὶ τὸ ὀψάριον ὁμοίως. [14]τοῦτο ἤδη τρίτον ἐφανερώθη Ἰησοῦς τοῖς μαθηταῖς ἐγερθεὶς ἐκ νεκρῶν.

EXERCISES FOR
INFINITIVES & PARTICIPLES

For each of the following words, write the stem, the ending, and the "tense" of the infinitive. Do it as in the example:

Example:

λῦσαι	λυ-	-σαι	aorist

ἀπίστευσαι

χάρσειν

κράζειν

λύσειν

πρόλεξαι

δίκαιουν

κράσαι

λύειν

πρόλεξειν

ἀπίστευειν

χαίρειν

δίκαιοσειν

κράσειν

ἀπίστευσειν

χάρσαι

δίκαιοσαι

πρόλεγειν

Here are all the verbs that you have memorized (hopefully!). Using the dictionary, find the present infinitive form for all of them.

ἄγω	ζητέω
αἴρω	φανερόω
αἰτέω	θέλω
ἀγαπάω	καλύπτω
ἀκολουθέω	κελεύω
ἀκούω	κηρύσσω
ἀνοίγω	κράζω
ἀπιστέω	κρίνω
ἀποκρίνομαι	λαλέω
ἀποκτείνω	λεγω
ἀποθνήσκω	λύω
ἀποστέλλω	μετανοέω
βαπτίζο	μένω
βλέπω	ὀφείλω
γινώσκω	πάσχω
γίνομαι	πειράζω
γράφω	πείθω
διδάσκω	περιπατέω
δικαιόω	πέμπω
δίδωμι	πληρόω
διώκω	ποιέω
δύναμαι	πορεύομαι
ἔχω	προλέγω
ἐγείρω	προσεύχομαι
ἐλεέω	σώζω
ἐλπίζω	τηρέω
ἐσθίω	ὑποστρέφω
εἰμί	χαίρω
εὐχαριστέω	χαίρω
εὑρίσκω	

Translate the following phrases into Greek:

Seeing is believing.

the giving mother

to the loving father

Hearing the truth is good.

Sending the men was good.

God sent the baptizing disciples.

knowing the truth

Peter gave the writing to me.

We are hoping.

We will be praising.

Finding the bread was good.

living in the light

Wishing is not living.

The truth is revealing.

We love preaching the Word.

Judging men is not good.

repenting of our sins

We are remaining in the light.

The words of God are fulfilling.

praying always

saving faith

We are rejoicing in the Son.

Translate the following sentences into English:

Καὶ εὖρεν ἐν τῷ ἱερῷ τοὺς πωλοῦντας βόας καὶ πρόβατα καὶ περιστερὰς καὶ τοὺς κερματιστὰς καθημένους. (John 2:14)

Ην δὲ καὶ ὁ Ἰωάννης βαπτίζων ἐν Αἰνὼν ἐγγὺς τοῦ Σαλείμ. (John 3:23)

ἀπεκρίθη Ἰωάννης καὶ εἶπεν, οὐ δύναται ἄνθρωπος λαμβάνειν οὐδὲ ἓν ἐὰν μὴ ᾖ δεδομένον αὐτῷ ἐκ τοῦ οὐρανοῦ. (John 3:27)

ὁ λαβὼν αὐτοῦ τὴν μαρτυρίαν ἐσφράγισεν ὅτι ὁ θεὸς ἀληθής ἐστιν. (John 3:33)

διὰ τοῦτο οὖν μᾶλλον ἐζήτουν αὐτὸν οἱ Ἰουδαῖοι ἀποκτεῖναι, ὅτι οὐ μόνον ἔλυεν τὸ σάββατον, ἀλλὰ καὶ πατέρα ἴδιον ἔλεγεν τὸν θεὸν ἴσον ἑαυτὸν ποιῶν τῷ θεῷ. (John 5:14)

Ἀμὴν ἀμὴν λέγω ὑμῖν ὅτι ὁ τὸν λόγον μου ἀκούων καὶ πιστεύων τῷ πέμψαντί με ἔχει ζωὴν αἰώνιον καὶ εἰς κρίσιν οὐκ ἔρχεται, ἀλλὰ μεταβέβηκεν ἐκ τοῦ θανάτου εἰς τὴν ζωήν. (John 5:24)

Translate the following sentences into Greek:

Seeing Peter, James called out to him.

The holy sisters rejoiced to know the Lord Jesus.

The prophets warned the crowd so that they would not sin.

The mystery of the gospel is Jesus; knowing him is life and light.

Not believing the Gospel is a sin; it is good to pity people in this sin.

The women, telling the children to remain, found bread in the house.

Opening the synagogue, the scribes and Pharisees found Jesus teaching
the people.

The disciples went to the Temple and saw the sisters praying there.

The soldiers guarding Paul did not believe the gospel.

God asks us to suffer for Christ.

Here is John 8:30-42. You should have little trouble identifying the parts of speech. Any new words can be found in the dictionary. We'll wind up our study of Greek with this passage; you can work on it for this lesson and the next one. Have fun!

Ταῦτα αὐτοῦ λαλοῦντος πολλοὶ ἐπίστευσαν εἰς αὐτόν. ³¹ἔλεγεν οὖν ὁ

Ἰησοῦς πρὸς τοὺς πεπιστευκότας αὐτῷ Ἰουδαίους, ἐὰν

ὑμεῖς μείνητε ἐν τῷ λόγῳ τῷ ἐμῷ, ἀληθῶς μαθηταί μού ἐστε ³²καὶ γνώσεσθε

τὴν ἀλήθειαν, καὶ ἡ ἀλήθεια ἐλευθερώσει ὑμᾶς.

³³ἀπεκρίθησαν πρὸς αὐτόν, σπέρμα Ἀβραάμ ἐσμεν καὶ οὐδενὶ

δεδουλεύκαμεν πώποτε, πῶς σὺ λέγεις ὅτι ἐλεύθεροι γενήσεσθε

³⁴ἀπεκρίθη αὐτοῖς ὁ Ἰησοῦς, ἀμὴν ἀμὴν λέγω ὑμῖν ὅτι πᾶς ὁ

ποιῶν τὴν ἁμαρτίαν δοῦλός ἐστιν τῆς ἁμαρτίας. ³⁵ὁ δὲ δοῦλος

οὐ μένει ἐν τῇ οἰκίᾳ εἰς τὸν αἰῶνα, ὁ υἱὸς μένει εἰς τὸν αἰῶνα.

³⁶ἐὰν οὖν ὁ υἱὸς ὑμᾶς ἐλευθερώσῃ, ὄντως ἐλεύθεροι ἔσεσθε.

³⁷Οἶδα ὅτι σπέρμα Ἀβραάμ ἐστε, ἀλλὰ ζητεῖτέ με ἀποκτεῖναι,

ὅτι ὁ λόγος ὁ ἐμὸς οὐ χωρεῖ ἐν ὑμῖν. ³⁸ἃ ἐγὼ ἑώρακα παρὰ τῷ

πατρὶ λαλῶ, καὶ ὑμεῖς οὖν ἃ ἠκούσατε παρὰ τοῦ πατρὸς ποιεῖτε.

³⁹ἀπεκρίθησαν καὶ εἶπαν αὐτῷ, ὁ πατὴρ ἡμῶν ᾿Αβραάμ ἐστιν.

λέγει αὐτοῖς ὁ ᾿Ιησοῦς, εἰ τέκνα τοῦ ᾿Αβραάμ ἐστε, τὰ ἔργα τοῦ᾿

Αβραὰμ ἐποιεῖτε, ⁴⁰νῦν δὲ ζητεῖτέ με ἀποκτεῖναι ἄνθρωπον ὃς

τὴν ἀλήθειαν ὑμῖν λελάληκα ἣν ἤκουσα παρὰ τοῦ θεοῦ, τοῦτο

᾿Αβραὰμ οὐκ ἐποίησεν. ⁴¹ὑμεῖς ποιεῖτε τὰ ἔργα τοῦ πατρὸς ὑμῶν.

εἶπαν οὖν αὐτῷ, ἡμεῖς ἐκ πορνείας οὐ γεγεννήμεθα, ἕνα πατέρα ἔχομεν τὸν

θεόν. ⁴²εἶπεν αὐτοῖς ὁ ᾿Ιησοῦς, εἰ ὁ θεὸς πατὴρ ὑμῶν

ἦν ἠγαπᾶτε ἂν ἐμέ, ἐγὼ γὰρ ἐκ τοῦ θεοῦ ἐξῆλθον καὶ ἥκω.

EXERCISES FOR
VERB CHART – ODDBALL VERBS

For each of the following words, write the stem, person, number, tense and meaning. Do it as in the example:

Example:

	stem:	person:	number:	tense:	meaning:
δίδωμι	διδο-	1st	s.	Present	I give
δίδομεν					
δίδως					
ἵστασαν					
ἵστης					
τίθει					
δίδωσιν					
ἵσταμεν					
ἵστησιν					
ἵδοτε					
τίθεμεν					
ἐδίδουν					
ἵστατε					
ἵστην					
ἱδόασιν					
τίθετε					
ἐδίδου					
ἐτίθεσαν					
ἵστης					
ἱστᾶσιν					
τίθης					
ἐδίδομεν					
ἵστη					
τίθεμεν					
τίθησιν					
ἐδίδοτε					
ἵσταμεν					
τίθην					
τίθετε					
ἐδίδοσαν					
ἔτιθεις					
ἵστατε					
τιθέασιν					

For each of the following words, write the stem, person, number, tense and meaning. Do it as in the example:

Example:

	stem:	person:	number:	tense:	meaning:
γίνωμαι	γινο-	1st	s.	Present	I become

ἐλεύσεσθε
ἐρχόμεθα
γενήσεται
γίνῃ
λήμψονται
ἐλεῦσονται
ἔρχεσθε
γενησόμεθα
γίνεται
γνώσομαι
ἔρχονται
γένησεσθε
γινόμεθα
γνῶσῃ
λήμψομαι
ἐλεῦσομαι
γενήσονται
γίνεσθε
γνώσεται
λημίψῃ
ἐλεῦσῃ
ἔρχομαι
γίνονται
γνωσόμεθα
λημίψεται
ἐλεῦσεται
ἔρχῃ
γενήσομαι
γνώσεσθε
λημψόμεθα
ἐλεῦσομεθα
ἔρχεται
γένησῃ
γνώσονται
λήμψεσθε

Translate the following phrases into Greek:

he fulfilled
I will love
we did
you (pl) did
you (s) fulfilled
I will honor
she will fulfill
they will do
we will fulfill
you (pl) will do
you (s) will love
he will love
they did
we fulfilled
you (pl) fulfilled
you (s) honored
I did
she will honor
they will fulfill
we will love
you (pl) will fulfill
you (s) will honor
he honored
I will do
they fulfilled
we honored
you (pl) will love
you (s) will do
I fulfilled
she did
they will love
we will honor
you (s) did
he will do
I will fulfill
we will do
you (pl) honored
you (s) will fulfill

Translate the following sentences into English:

ὅσοι δὲ ἔλαβον αὐτόν, ἔδωκεν αὐτοῖς ἐξουσίαν τέκνα θεοῦ γενέσθαι, τοῖς πιστεύουσιν εἰς τὸ ὄνομα αὐτοῦ, ¹³οἳ οὐκ ἐξ αἱμάτων οὐδὲ ἐκ θελήματος σαρκὸς οὐδὲ ἐκ θελήματος ἀνδρὸς ἀλλ ἐκ θεοῦ ἐγεννήθησαν. (John 1:12-13)

οὕτως γὰρ ἠγάπησεν ὁ θεὸς τὸν κόσμον, ὥστε τὸν υἱὸν τὸν μονογενῆ ἔδωκεν, ἵνα πᾶς ὁ πιστεύων εἰς αὐτὸν μὴ ἀπόληται ἀλλ ἔχῃ ζωὴν αἰώνιον. (John 3:16)

εἰ δὲ ποιῶ, κἂν ἐμοὶ μὴ πιστεύητε, τοῖς ἔργοις πιστεύετε, ἵνα γνῶτε καὶ γινώσκητε ὅτι ἐν ἐμοὶ ὁ πατὴρ κἀγὼ ἐν τῷ πατρί. (John 10:38)

ἀλλ ἵνα πληρωθῇ ὁ λόγος ὁ ἐν τῷ νόμῳ αὐτῶν γεγραμμένος ὅτι ἐμίσησαν με δωρεάν. (John 15:25)

Μὴ νομίσητε ὅτι ἦλθον καταλῦσαι τὸν νόμον ἢ τοὺς προφήτας, οὐκ ἦλθον καταλῦσαι ἀλλὰ πληρῶσαι. (Matthew 5:17)

Translate the following sentences into Greek:

We love to fulfill the word of Christ.

The authority of the disciples will become the joy of the Church.

The soldiers put the garments on Peter and led him to the prison.

Honor your father and your mother.

To know and to believe is the good work from God.

The evil men will receive power from hated demons.

I will stand in the light from Heaven so that I might live.

The disciples fulfilled the commandments of Christ, in order to fulfill the love of God.

Men will come from the synagogue, giving bread to the crowd.

Take salvation from the hand of Christ, so that you might see God.

Here again is John 8:30-42. You should be able to finish it up now.

Ταῦτα αὐτοῦ λαλοῦντος πολλοὶ ἐπίστευσαν εἰς αὐτόν. [31]ἔλεγεν οὖν ὁ

Ἰησοῦς πρὸς τοὺς πεπιστευκότας αὐτῷ Ἰουδαίους, ἐὰν

ὑμεῖς μείνητε ἐν τῷ λόγῳ τῷ ἐμῷ, ἀληθῶς μαθηταί μού ἐστε [32]καὶ γνώσεσθε

τὴν ἀλήθειαν, καὶ ἡ ἀλήθεια ἐλευθερώσει ὑμᾶς.

[33]ἀπεκρίθησαν πρὸς αὐτόν, σπέρμα Ἀβραάμ ἐσμεν καὶ οὐδενὶ

δεδουλεύκαμεν πώποτε, πῶς σὺ λέγεις ὅτι ἐλεύθεροι γενήσεσθε

[34]ἀπεκρίθη αὐτοῖς ὁ Ἰησοῦς, ἀμὴν ἀμὴν λέγω ὑμῖν ὅτι πᾶς ὁ

ποιῶν τὴν ἁμαρτίαν δοῦλός ἐστιν τῆς ἁμαρτίας. [35]ὁ δὲ δοῦλος

οὐ μένει ἐν τῇ οἰκίᾳ εἰς τὸν αἰῶνα, ὁ υἱὸς μένει εἰς τὸν αἰῶνα.

[36]ἐὰν οὖν ὁ υἱὸς ὑμᾶς ἐλευθερώσῃ, ὄντως ἐλεύθεροι ἔσεσθε.

[37]Οἶδα ὅτι σπέρμα Ἀβραάμ ἐστε, ἀλλὰ ζητεῖτέ με ἀποκτεῖναι,

ὅτι ὁ λόγος ὁ ἐμὸς οὐ χωρεῖ ἐν ὑμῖν. [38]ἃ ἐγὼ ἑώρακα παρὰ τῷ

πατρὶ λαλῶ, καὶ ὑμεῖς οὖν ἃ ἠκούσατε παρὰ τοῦ πατρὸς ποιεῖτε.

[39]ἀπεκρίθησαν καὶ εἶπαν αὐτῷ, ὁ πατὴρ ἡμῶν Ἀβραάμ ἐστιν.

λέγει αὐτοῖς ὁ Ἰησοῦς, εἰ τέκνα τοῦ Ἀβραάμ ἐστε, τὰ ἔργα τοῦ

Ἀβραὰμ ἐποιεῖτε, ⁴⁰νῦν δὲ ζητεῖτέ με ἀποκτεῖναι ἄνθρωπον ὃς

τὴν ἀλήθειαν ὑμῖν λελάληκα ἣν ἤκουσα παρὰ τοῦ θεοῦ, τοῦτο

Ἀβραὰμ οὐκ ἐποίησεν. ⁴¹ὑμεῖς ποιεῖτε τὰ ἔργα τοῦ πατρὸς ὑμῶν.

εἶπαν οὖν αὐτῷ, ἡμεῖς ἐκ πορνείας οὐ γεγεννήμεθα, ἕνα πατέρα ἔχομεν τὸν

θεόν. ⁴²εἶπεν αὐτοῖς ὁ Ἰησοῦς, εἰ ὁ θεὸς πατὴρ ὑμῶν

ἦν ἠγαπᾶτε ἂν ἐμέ, ἐγὼ γὰρ ἐκ τοῦ θεοῦ ἐξῆλθον καὶ ἥκω.

NOTES

NOTES

www.ingramcontent.com/pod-product-compliance
Lightning Source LLC
Chambersburg PA
CBHW080506110426
42742CB00017B/3010